W9-BWP-931

The First Freudians

The First Freudians

Edited and with an Introduction
by Hendrik M. Ruitenbeek, Ph.D.

Jason Aronson, Inc.　　　　　New York

For M. Masud R. Khan

Contents

The First Freudians

Introduction

Hendrik M. Ruitenbeek

The pioneers of psychoanalysis were an interesting lot. Since most of them, by virtue of being the first ones, were not professionally trained in psychoanalysis, they were able to exhibit a rather relaxed and creative attitude towards the practice and study of psychoanalysis.

Contemporary psychoanalysts, in contrast, lack the broad cultural knowledge the early psychoanalysts in many ways possessed, and have shown less creativity as well. Let us remember, however, that the first Freudians did not spend their early years in long and arduous training, meeting the demanding standards of educational committees and involved in the ambitious training analyses lasting many years that are required today. Currently many analysts lose the creative years of their thirties in training and do not start their pschoanalytic practice until they are forty. Moreover, contemporary analysts have ignored Freud's warning that psychoanalysis is not a branch of medicine and that it depends very heavily upon the creative resources of other disciplines such as philosophy, sociology, cultural history, and anthropology.

The first Freudians were examples of the creative and imaginative analysts we so desperately need in psychoanalysis today. Otto Rank was a novelist, poet, and philosopher and drew heavily upon the resources of ancient literature and history in the analysis of his patients. Hanns Sachs, the learned and erudite editor of *Imago,* was trained as a lawyer and devoted a lifetime in establishing important links between psychoanalysis and the other disciplines. Even the medically trained analysts, not in the least Freud himself, were examples of men who did not restrict themselves to a narrow discipline but had a broad and often intimate knowledge with philosophy, religion, sociology, and the literature of their times. It is not a surprise that many of Freud's intimates and correspondents were to be found among the literary giants of his time such as Thomas Mann, Romain Rolland, and Stefan Zweig.

A number of years ago, I had the opportunity to read through the *Rundbriefe* (the early correspondence of the principal members of the International Psychoanalytic Association) and I was struck by how interesting was the group of people surrounding Freud during the first decades of psychoanalysis.[1] Fortunately, more and more is being learned about the ideas of Freud's early followers and the character of the relationships which existed between them and Freud, as well as among themselves. Ernest Jones has given us a memorable series of portraits of Freud's entourage. The publication of the minutes of the Vienna Psychoanalytic Society (the celebrated "Wednesday" meetings) and the newly-published translation of Lou Andreas-Salomé's notes have given us further glimpses of what was taking place in the early years of psychoanalysis. Much information is still to come. Unfortunately, not all the early outstanding analytic pioneers have recorded their experiences. Too often, their correspondence is guarded by over-anxious literary executors who do small service to the historian of psychoanalysis by their zeal. Much important German and Viennese material was lost during World War II, of course, but much still remains to be discovered and made available both to scholars and to the educated public.

Freud and his students (disciples might be a more apt term) were brought together by the conviction that they were making history as well as by their shared interest. Certainly, we find pettiness and small-mindedness among these people, as we find in all human relationships, but there was also a sense of dedication to something larger and more important than personal

---

[1]Part of the *Rundbriefe* will be published in *Freud's Circle,* a book I am preparing for publication by Delacorte Press, New York.

ambition or personal glory. As Lou Andreas-Salomé wrote:[2]

> Freud also talked about why I had become so deeply involved
> in psychoanalysis. To begin with, it was nothing but the
> kind of neutral objective interest that one feels when embark-
> ing on new researches. Then the opportunity came in all its
> liveliness and personal urgency to stand in the presence of a
> new science, again and again to be at a beginning and thus
> related to the problems of the science in an increasingly inti-
> mate way. What settled the matter for me, however, was the
> third and most personal reason, that psychoanalysis bestowed
> a gift on me personally, its radiant enrichment of my own
> life from slowly groping to the roots by which it is embedded
> in the totality.

Freud's immediate heirs, as pioneers and defenders of a new
discipline were, naturally, beset by all the problems of pioneers
and showed all the deficiencies of their position: rigidity in
adhering to the cause; inflexibility; reluctance to accept reinterpre-
tation of the introduction of new ideas about psychoanalysis.
Because the group was small and its ideas revolutionary, individuals became deeply involved; envy was evident among them
and often there were indications of instability or even actual
emotional disturbance.[3] All this colors the writings of Freud's
heirs. They had not learned how—to use the literary term—
to *distance* themselves from their master. When they did achieve
real distance, they ran the chance of expulsion from the psychoanalytic movement proper. Let us not forget that not all of
Freud's followers were Jungs or Adlers. Too much emphasis is
sometimes placed on those among his disciples who ultimately
produced ideas on the structure and application of psychoanalysis
which were at total variance with Freud's. I have always thought

---

[2]*The Freud Journal of Lou Andreas-Salome* (New York: Basic Books,
1964), pp. 89-90.

---

[3]It is by now common knowledge that some of the early analysts were
at times highly disturbed, if not psychotic. This did not necessarily,
however, make them less effective as analysts.

that, in terms of analytic theory and its applications, there is much of value to be found among those analytic pioneers who did not significantly deviate from Freud. In their continuation and elaboration of his basic theory, Freud's non-divergent successors make their greatest claim on our attention. Some of the people represented in this book belonged to the inner-most circle of Freud's co-workers; others were not part of that specially favored group. Yet they, too, made significant contributions to psychoanalytic theory.

It is difficult to rank the authors of these essays on a scale of closeness to Freud or to his thinking. Ernest Jones will always be remembered as Freud's biographer; during Freud's life, Jones was very much the protector and interpreter of Freud's teaching and thought. His loyalty was unswerving. The quality of his personal relationship with Freud is difficult to ascertain since it is so much in dispute among others of the Freud circle. Certainly, Jones' most significant contribution is to the organization and maintenance of the psychoanalytic movement rather than to the growth of psychoanalytic thought.

Sándor Ferenczi is certainly one of the most illustrious figures of the early decades of psychoanalysis. His contributions to analytic theory are of great importance. His influence upon post- and neo-Freudian thinking has been equally important. To no small extent, he influenced the founders of the William Alanson White school and, until his tragic illness and death, Clara Thompson was one of Ferenczi's closest friends and supporters. Although Ferenczi's important contributions to the development of psychoanalytic technique have been recognized, his work on sexuality has been too little regarded by contemporary psychoanalysts. *Thalassa,* his beautiful and illuminating book on genitality, has, unfortunately, been all but ignored. As an analytic technician, Ferenczi favored the therapist's taking a more active role than Freud recommended:[4]

Active technique rouses certain activities in the patient, inhibi-

---

[4]Sandor Ferenczi, *Further Contributions to the Theory and Technique of Psychoanalysis* (New York: Basic Books, 1952), p. 212.

tions, psychic discrepancies, or a discharge of affect, and expects *secondarily* the accessibility of the unconscious or of the memory material. In any event, the activity roused in the patient is only means to the end, while the discharge of affect in catharsis was regarded as an end in itself. Where then the task of catharsis ends, the real work of the "active" analyst only begins.

Freud and Ferenczi remained on friendly terms until Ferenczi's death, but Freud did not agree with his new departures. The essence of their differences lay in divergent ideas about the role of infantile trauma and parental unkindness in producing neurosis. Ferenczi thought lack of love to be basic in generating neurotic attitudes. In order to neutralize the early unhappiness of the patient, the analyst, Ferenczi thought, should assume the posture of the loving parent. This implied a tender relationship. Instead of acting as the neutral mirror, the analyst might even go so far as to accept analysis of himself by his analysand.

Freud was keenly aware of the dangers inherent in the Ferenczi approach. Analysis was in sufficient danger of attack for giving rein to quackery without laying itself open to the charge of encouraging indiscreet, if not immoral, behavior. As Freud wrote:[5]

I see that the differences between us come to a head in a technical detail which is well worth discussing. You have not made a secret of the fact that you kiss your patients and let them kiss you; I had also heard that from a patient of my own. Now when you decide to give a full acount of your technique and its results you will have to choose between two ways: either you relate this or you conceal it. The latter, as you may well think, is dishonorable. What one does in one's technique one has to defend openly. . . . Now I am assuredly not one of those who from prudishness or from consideration of bourgeoise convention would condemn little erotic gratifications of this kind. And I am also aware that in the time of the

---

[5]Ernest Jones, *Life and Work of Sigmund Freud* (New York: Basic Books, 1957), III, 163-164.

Nibelungs a kiss was a harmless greeting granted to every guest. . . . Now picture what will be the result of publishing your technique. There is no revolutionary who is not driven out of the field by a still more radical one. A number of independent thinkers in matters of technique will say to themselves: why stop at a kiss? . . . and soon we shall have accepted in the technique of analysis the whole repetoire of *demi-viergerie* and petting parties.

Nevertheless, he continued to be on good terms with Ferenczi. He described Ferenczi's death as a "great and painful" loss, personal and professional. Some of Ferenczi's American pupils, notably Izette de Forest, maintain that Freud acted harshly.[6] Jones, on the other hand, insists that there is no basis for their charge.[7]

Karl Abraham was considered the most stable, normal person in the pioneer group. Next to Ferenczi, he was, in Ernest Jones' opinion, the most effective analyst. Jones describes Abraham as intellectually independent and emotionally self-contained. Within the group of intimates, he struck no particular alliances. "He was not closer to any one of us than to the others," Jones writes,[8] and from that sentence one can infer a whole atmosphere of cliquish rivalry, half endearing, half childish, and, to an unsympathetic eye, all a bit absurd. Abraham's contributions to psychoanalytic theory were sound, although they lack the poetic brilliance which characterizes Ferenczi. Abraham's work on melancholia, which Freud singled out, continues to be useful to both the clinician and the student of human behavior.

Another important member of the inner circle was Max Eitingon, the only one among the first analysts who had considerable independent means. He was thus able to give the psychoanalytic movement financial support, notably, to keep its publishing house a going concern. Since psychoanalytic studies were by no means acceptable to the editors of medical and

---

[6]Izette de Forest, *The Leaven of Love* (New York: Harper and Brothers, 1954).
[7]Jones, *op. cit.,* III, 176.
[8]*Ibid.,* II, 159,

psychological journals, and since few, if any, publishers would risk doing books on psychoanalysis, Eitingon's access to funds was crucially important in circulating Freudian theory and getting it a hearing in intellectual circles. Eitingon's contributions to the theory of psychoanalysis were less significant than those of some of Freud's other intimates, but he was an active participant in the pioneer discussions and wrote many papers. His contribution to this volume deals with the problem of lay analysis, an issue which still troubles professional waters. Particularly in the United States, where the practice of medicine continues to be organized as an independent business of a nineteenth-century type, one may question the relevance of medical training for the psychoanalyst who finds himself more and more compelled to attend to his patients' societal problems. Such issues did not confront the pioneers in psychoanalysis, however; they found the demand that analysts have medical training to be one means, and often a useful one, of protecting the professional standards of a new discipline.

Hanns Sachs played one of the least controversial roles in the group of analysts gathered around Freud. Sachs continued faithful to Freud until his last days and all but refused to become involved in disputation. Sachs was a rather aloof person and avoided the clash of individual temperaments. He concentrated on the relationship between psychoanalysis and art and wrote brilliantly on his chosen subject. Later, he emigrated to the United States where he devoted himself to analytic practice and the training of analysts. With Freud's permission and encouragement, Sachs founded the American *Imago* after the German publication was silenced by the rise of Hitler. Not long before Freud's death, Sachs visited him to "take what he knew would be his last leave of the man he called 'master and friend'." He was, Jones noted, particularly struck by two facts: Freud was in pain but he showed no sign of complaint or irritability; he was fully aware of his fate and fully resigned to it. He continued to be interested in what was happening to the psychoanalytic movement in the United States and kept informed about people and events in analytic circles there.[9]

---

[9]*Ibid.*, III, 244-245.
[10]*Internationale Zeitschrift für Psychoanalyse,* XVIII (1932), 265.

Eduard Hitschmann was undoubtedly outstanding among the Freudian adherents. He had been associated with psychoanalysis from the beginning. He generally attended the "Wednesdays" and, together with Paul Federn and Helene Deutsch, was the founder of the Vienna psychoanalytic clinic. He encountered many difficulties in establishing the institution, the *Ambulatorium,* as it was called. The Viennese authorities did not . approve of it, and although they allowed it to open in May, 1922, they closed it six months later; but it was finally reopened. Hitschmann has described his experiences in "Zehn Jahre Wiener Psychoanalytisches Ambulatorium,"[10] where one sees in vivid detail how difficult it was to conduct a center for analytic therapy in the city where that therapy was born. Hitschmann did not participate in the controversies among Freud's intimates, an abstention which made it easier for him to continue an untroubled relationship with Freud. Besides offering psychoanalytic interpretations of a number of historical and literary personages, Hitschmann was interested in what is today called parapsychology. He wrote a number of essays on the relationship between the phenomena which are labeled occult, and the psychoanalytic concept of the nature of the personality.

To anyone even slightly familiar with Freud's life, Marie Bonaparte scarcely needs an introduction. It was largely to her intervention that the world owes the relatively peaceful continuance of that life after Hitler invaded and annexed Austria, for she was among those whose efforts made it possible for Freud to escape. Marie Bonaparte did not become acquainted with Freud until psychoanalysis was a fairly mature discipline, but she became a loyal supporter of his ideas and a good friend. Indeed, along with his wife, his daughter Anna, and Lou Andreas-Salomé, Marie Bonaparte is one of the four important women in his life. But she is a significant psychoanalyst in her own right: she wrote illuminatingly about female sexuality and her study of Edgar Allan Poe continues unsurpassed.

Helene Deutsch and Melanie Klein are two of the other women who figured notably in the early history of psychoanalysis. Along with Hitschmann, Helene Deutsch was instrumental in setting up the first psychoanalytic clinic in Vienna. She was especially active in the training institute of the Viennese Psychoanalytic Society and so may be termed a kind of "grandmother" of analysis. She, however, helped to formulate the lore she passed along. Her contribution to our understanding of the psychological development of women is still exerting influence.

Melanie Klein is perhaps more closely associated with Ferenczi than with Freud himself, but her pioneering work in child analysis seems Freudian in technique if not in interpretation. She considered it possible to avoid the didactic approach in play therapy and her description of her relationship with child patients shows her to be free, in appearance at least, of any tinge of Ferenczi's willingness to treat his patients in a dangerously affectionate manner. Freud did not see eye to eye with Klein's work in child analysis, and Jones is willing to suggest that Freud's attitude was not unconnected with Anna Freud's interest in and concern with the same area of interest.

Anna Freud, whose essay appears last in this book, did more than follow creditably in her father's footsteps. She introduced new and brilliant concepts in psychoanalysis. Her contribution to the understanding of child development is well-known. Her work on the ego and on defense mechanisms should be considered classic.

Two Americans, A. A. Brill and James Putnam, are to be considered among Freud's heirs. Putnam was one of the earliest supporters of Freud in the United States. He wrote extensively on psychoanalytic theory and technique although he did not produce any notable large-scale systematic work. Although Putnam later came to differ with Freud, his acceptance of Freud's early work was especially important in that time of rebuff and discouragement. Putnam helped introduce Freud to Americans and thus must be counted among those who assisted materially in the dissemination of psychoanalytic thinking. Unlike Putnam, Brill remained a loyally orthodox Freudian to the end. Although his translations are now superseded, they were useful in their time. As an organizer and administrator, Brill played a leading part in making the practice of psychoanalysis a respectable profession in the United States.

Another of the people constantly present at Freud's "Wednesdays" was Paul Federn. Although he does not have the stature of a Ferenczi or an Abraham, he made some minor contributions to analytic thought. After Freud became too ill for active service as an executive, Federn took his seat as President of the Viennese Psychoanalytic Society, serving until 1938, when the society had to be dissolved.

Hartmann and Wälder may almost be called a second generation among Freud's heirs although their ties with Freud and his contemporary intimates were close indeed. Hartmann is best known for developing the theory of ego psychology. Wälder served as editor of *Imago* for a long time. Franz Alexander should certainly be considered among the second generation of Freud's heirs, but his work—also in ego psychology—entitles him to a place in this collection.

II

The essays chosen for this collection show the continuous concern for analytic technique and theory which pervaded the work of the pioneers. Although most of them were written a long time ago, I think that they retain their significance for furthering our understanding of the psychoanalytic process. Ferenczi's article is more descriptive than theoretical or clinical but it helps us see how one of the pioneer analysts regarded the relationship between psychoanalysis and medicine.

Jones' essay on the origin and structure of the superego continues to be useful for helping us comprehend the significance of that structure in psychoanalysis. The relationship between metaphysics and analysis has never ben explored in depth. James Putnam's essay retains its first imperative ring, therefore, as it calls on persons familiar with both disciplines to examine each field in the other's light.

The question "Shall we have patients write down their dreams" which Karl Abraham discusses, seems pertinent since many contemporary analysts believe that we should. It certainly appears worthwhile to weigh the views of so experienced and brilliant a practitioner as Abraham.

Brill's essay on sexuality as a factor in neurosis, although an eloquent restatement of the orthodox Freudian approach, still throws new light on old questions. Hanns Sachs' case history of the wish to be a man retains a high degree of contemporary relevance because of the many instances of role and sex confusion which therapists continue to see among their patients.

After nearly half a century of clinical practice and of dispute, the problem of lay analysis is still unresolved. Several associations of American psychoanalysts make the medical degree a prerequisite for psychoanalytic training and professional acceptance. This insistence seems to ignore the realities of the situation. Medical schools in the United States are currently training fewer doctors than the number optimally required to deal with the merely physical ills of a rising population. Further, the administrators of those schoools are asserting that they no longer get the ablest undergraduates as applicants for admission. On the other hand, studies of mental health and mental illness make it clear that we need increasing numbers of adequately prepared psychotherapists. The patients' prospects seem bleak indeed if the psychoanalytic "establishment" continues to demand that the medical schools be the sole suppliers of candidates for analytic training and to banish all but the exceptional lay analyst as un-Freudian. Freud's own position was far less rigid than that of our contemporaries. Eitingon's essay restates some of the relevant issues involved in lay versus medical analysis.

As observed earlier, Edward Hitschmann was among the first analysts to deal seriously with parapsychology. Contemporary analysts like Fedor and Ehrenwald have treated phenomena like poltergeists and extrasensory perception. Hitschmann's essay on telepathy shows that psychoanalysts have long had an interest in the possible relationship between the operation of unconscious factors in the personality and the appearance of phenomena which have been taken as the work of occult powers. Today, as in the past, patients have been intrigued by dreams of flying, and it seems appropriate to read Paul Federn on interpreting this type of dream. The interpretation of dreams continues to be a significant element in the contemporary practice of psychotherapy whether it be strictly Freudian or a departure from orthodoxy.

Anna Freud and Melanie Klein both deal with problems of child analysis. Anna Freud is concerned with developing a general approach; Melanie Klein writes about one of the most generally significant aspects of child development: the growth of conscience. Since conscience and its pricks are a main sanction of morality, whatever makes it possible for us to deepen our understanding of how conscience appears and how it acquires content may make it more feasible for us to develop more useful and more trustworthy methods of psychological education.

Problems related to sado-masochism have always been considered difficult to deal with in the analytic situation. Rereading Marie Bonaparte's observations on the biopsychical aspects of sado-masochism seems the more relevant because contemporary psychoanalytic discussion all but ignores these aspects of the problem. Both Wälder and Helene Deutsch deal with immediate clinical problems in psychotherapeutic practice. Resistance expresses itself in so many forms that it sometimes becomes hard to trace. Discussion by a keen observer and a person experienced in practice is doubly useful; it serves to remind the therapist of things he may know so well that he forgets to notice them; it helps the lay reader appreciate the complexities of his own behavior in everyday life. Since both freedom and reality in the analytic situation are fundamental in creating the conditions for a successful analysis, Wälder's essay has lost nothing of its original importance.

Franz Alexander's essay defends and explains ego-psychology, which has become increasingly important among post-Freudian psychoanalysts. Another outstanding analyst and ego psychologist, Heinz Hartmann, deals with the concept of health and psychoanalysis. It seems plausible that psychoanalysis must somehow have affected our conception of what constitutes mental health, and perhaps the converse has also occurred, so that the state of mental health existing among the population may affect the interests and the direction of psychoanalytic therapy.

Freud's work, often challenged and occasionally even pronounced obsolete, continues to influence contemporary psychotherapy. In the welter of argument and opinion, we may, however, lose sight of what Freud's contemporaries have to give us—whether we are practicing therapists or merely educated persons trying to improve our understanding of the species to which we belong. This collection of essays will, hopefully, make clear the relevance of much that Freud's followers had to say. It will also show that during the early decades of the development of psychoanalysis, analysts, although involved in a good deal of fruitless quarreling, had time for significant work.

All the papers included in this collection are by now considered to be historical, since they were written by the pioneer members of the psychoanalytic movement centered about Freud. All of them were printed in the *Internationale Zeitschrift für Psychoanalyse* and in the *International Journal of Psycho-Analysis,* and are here reprinted by permission. For the reader who desires complete source material, I have noted the various other publications in which these papers appeared, and where they were read, I have noted the date and place of the lecture.

In a historical anthology it is difficult to make the reference materials consistent. I have tried, in all cases, to give the latest American editions of all books and papers cited. Some of the papers were originally written in English, but in those which were translated, I have given the translator's name; where no translator was credited, I have noted this fact.

So far as Freud's works are concerned, I would have preferred to cite, in all instances, the *Complete Works,* but once the major writings are easily accessible to the general reader in a variety of popular editions, I have referred to them where possible.

Freud's influence on medicine

Sándor Ferenczi

If one wishes to discuss in a constructive manner the significance of a person to science or to a branch of it, it would be of importance to describe the state of the development of the science before that person appeared and also the changes taking place under his influence. But even such a description would hardly satisfy the deeper desire for causality. We would have to point out in detail whether existent material had merely been synthesized by a constructive mind or whether an intellectual light had, like a meteor, struck an unsuspecting and unprepared world. Finally, we cannot evade the question as to what degree chance and to what extent rare personal peculiarities are to be considered the decisive factors in the discovery of a new science and its formulation into theory. If the investigation has been carried up to this point, there still remains the task of supplementing the contributions with a kind of personality study.

To portray Freud's influence on medicine, I must limit myself to remarks on these problems, but above all, I must expound the accidental factors. Without doubt it was an accident that the otherwise well deserving Viennese physician, Dr. Josef Breuer, had an intelligent female patient under hypnotic treatment, who observed in herself the favorable effect of talking about the content of her fantasies and called her physician's attention to her observation. Literally, she is the discoverer of the original cathartic method. It was another casualty which later brought Sigmund Freud into personal contact with Breuer. But it certainly was no chance incident that Breuer, notwithstanding profound insight into the importance of the discovery from the psychological as well as from the pathological angle, soon discontinued interest in these problems and no longer associated himself with Freud or his further studies. It is no longer a secret to what qualities in him, Freud owes his perseverance and his results in the scientific development of psychoanalysis. Of these qualities I name his objectivity, which remained unaffected, even before the problems of sex. Strange as it sounds, it is nevertheless true that, before Freud, even those who considered themselves enlightened were not free of moral scruples in sex matters; they left untouched the psychological side of love life.

Only two courageous men dared, at least descriptively, to make the most repulsive peculiarities of sexual life the subject of an extensive study. These were the Viennese Krafft-Ebing and the Englishman Havelock Ellis, whose examples were soon followed by some German and Swiss scholars. The first attempts of Freud toward the explanation of Breuer's discovery soon led to the investigation of sexual problems. His friends and colleagues who recognized his genius only as long as he concerned himself with the moral, harmless questions about aphasia and cerebral infantile paralysis took to their heels and deserted him. Soon, even Breuer associated himself with those who did not wish to collaborate with Freud in his study of these unesthetic, hence unedifying things, and Freud stood alone. There began a period of his life which deserves to be called the heroic one and in which he produced the *Interpretation of Dreams*, the permanent foundation for all of his later ideas. Today, more than thirty years after its first publication, we still see the declining reaction of the rest of the world, which certainly points to the fact that psychoanalysis did not come up to the requirements of the scientific and medical world.

Another characteristic which predestined Freud to become the discoverer of psychoanalysis was his unrelenting criticism of the insufficiency of therapeutic ability and theoretical knowledge of that time, which evidenced itself in inadequacy and perplexity when dealing with neuroses. He became convinced of the futility of electrotherapy for the neuroses at a time when, almost like today, the faradic and galvanic apparatus was the chief weapon of the physician dealing with the so-called functional diseases. The transiency and unreliableness of the occasional results obtained by hypnotic and suggestive influence occasioned Freud to give up these methods. It would have been easy, particularly in the medical atmosphere in which he grew up, to accept the smug idea of medical nihilism, and to enjoy without a care his rapidly growing neurological practice. But through a specific trait in Freud, which included a zealous drive for truth which did not permit him to halt at mere criticism of the prevailing order of things, his inquisitive mind gave him no rest until the questions which he had once raised had been solved and that wholly without external aid. The work involved in this seemed insurmountable, for it was a matter of solving a problem with many unknowns. As Breuer and Freud already had recognized, the causes of neurotic symptoms were conjectured to lie in the unconscious psychic life, which is inaccessible to direct examination. As we have just mentioned, Freud deliberately dropped the methods of hypnosis and suggestion which permitted partial access to this unconscious system. He believed that, measured by the standard of psychological knowledge of the time, the efficacy of these methods must appear inexplicable or even mystical. Knowledge gathered through their application bears the marks of the mystical and does not meet the scientific requirement of clarity. Yet Freud had success with the improbable; the apparently unfathomable was exposed by his method of free association.

It is not easy to define the word genius, but I believe the term is appropriate to one who finds a solution to a hopeless situation of the sort outlined above. I do not hesitate to say that with this idea of Freud's, the future of psychology and all of its applications have been settled. It is no exaggeration to attribute to this idea, which arose in Freud's mind, all later developments in these sciences. Modern psychology was born at the moment Freud's main idea was conceived.

It was then necessary to sift the enormous amount of material which the new method had collected and to classify it scientifically. Whether for good or evil, Freud had soon to formulate a skeletal outline for his theory, a construction which, though it has been altered, modified, and remodeled many times, remains sound in its main details up to the present day. This construction is the so-called metapsychology. Briefly, I shall try to explain what we understand by this. Freud could not explain the origin of neurotic symptoms without imagining psychic functions in some spatial system where forces of certain intensity and quantity were interacting. The first topical division in psychic functions was the separation of the conscious and unconscious systems and the first idea of dynamics was that there was a conflict between the forces resident in each system. The outcome of this conflict depended on the economic relation between the two forces, yet the sum of the two psychic forces could practically always be considered constant. We need not be startled by the fact that the uninitiated regard this construction as fantastic; if one wished, he can call it a scientific fantasy. But every scientific theory is fantasy, and it is serviceable as such as long as it meets practical requirements and agrees with the facts of experience. Freud's metapsychologic system does this fully. It places us in the position to understand the disturbances in the psychic life of a patient as a result of such and similar conflicts, even in the position of favorably influencing the faulty distribution of those forces. Freud's later work caused the supersession of this very simple system with a much more complicated one. He was able to trace the motor force behind the psychic life to its biological source and to confirm its analogy with physical driving force. Leaving practical considerations aside, he did not permit himself to be led astray into denying the multiformity which manifested itself in this, nor did the illusion of a premature system of unification influence him to abandon his ideas which showed gaps, were not fully satisfactory, and yet were in accord with reality.

I do not hesitate to state that this construction of Freud's is in itself of the most important scientific significance. It means nothing less than the first attempt to solve something pertaining to the physics and physiology of psychic phenomena. The only means to this end was the penetrating psychoanalytic investigation into the psychic life of the sick and normal person. Up to this time, anatomy and physiology contributed absolutely no information about the finer psychic processes. Medical science stared rigidly, as if hypnotized, into the microscope and anticipated, from a knowledge of the development and the course of nerve fibers in the brain, the "how" of psychic functions. But these developments showed no more than the crudest facts about motor and sensory functions. Since no neurosis or functional psychosis revealed any changes in the brain, medical science was at a loss what to do about these pathologic conditions. The mistake lay in the fact that physicians before Freud's time were trained one-sidedly and materialistically. The striking psychic facts which play such an important role in our personal lives as well as in the lives of the patients were considered a kind of reality of minor importance to which no serious-minded scientist could apply himself. Psychology *per se* was abandoned and left to the dilettanti and belletrists. Timidity about unfounded generalization guarded Freud from the error of uniting prematurely the psychic and physical into materialistic monism, as was otherwise customary. His spirit of honesty prevailed on him to recognize the fact that psychic life was accessible only through introspective methods, that is, from the subjective side; further, that facts which become intelligible through subjective methods have full acceptance as to their psychic reality. Thus Freud became a dualist, a term which most physical scientists have regarded, and still regard, as almost opprobrious. I do not believe that Freud has scruples against the monistic conception of knowledge. His dualism only says that this unification is not possible at present, not in the near future, perhaps not completely unifiable at all. On no account should one confuse Freud's dualism with the naive separation of a living organism into a body and a mind. He is always mindful of the anatomic-physiological facts concerning the nervous system. He pursues his psychologic investigations up to the

point of the human impulses, which he comprehends as a
dividing line between the psychic and the physical, a line
which he does not believe psychologic interpretation should
cross, because it seems incompetent to do so. On the other
hand, just as his metapsychologic system, which is constructed on the pattern of the reflex arc, shows, even in his
pure psychologic investigations, he cannot dispense with
the analogies of natural science. To describe this form of
dualism, I must coin a new word, namely *ultraquism*, and
I believe that this method of investigation of natural as well
as mental science merits a great future.

One of the most remarkable things about the psychology
of Freud is that it not only writes down the content, i.e.,
a lexicon of the unconscious, but also formulates the rules
of peculiar grammar and primitive logic which reign there
so that the strange productions of the dream, the slips of
everyday life, and neurotic and psychotic symptoms become full of meaning and intelligible. You will admit that
a physician who understands the language of the psychotic
and neurotic patient and who can use it, so to speak, etio-
logically and etymologically, faces these sicknesses with a
very different understanding from that of the natural scientist who is little concerned about the origin of each individual phenomenon and who, in the treatment of this
condition, is guided exclusively by his artist-like intuition.
No one will wish to deny that even before Freud there
were distinguished psychotherapists, who in the treatment
of psychosis and neurosis were surprisingly clever and successful. But their art could not be learned; the fortunate
ones who possessed such talents could not, even with the
best intentions, give instruction in their manner of approach. In this contact between patient and physician, the
psychoanalyst would say that it was a dialogue between

two unconscious minds. The unconscious of the physician understood the unconscious of the patient and had then permitted the appropriate answer or idea of the proper remedy to arise in the physician's conscious mind. The progress which psychoanalysis signifies in medical practice is chiefly that, that out of this therapeutic art it has made a science which can be learned by every intelligent physician with as much ease or difficulty as he learns surgery or internal medicine. Naturally there will always be artists in psychoanalysis as there are in the other branches of healing. But presupposing the proper preparation and adherence to the instructions laid down by Freud in his works, there will be no obstacle in the way toward such training, even to the degree demanded of the specialist.

Those of practical disposition may become impatient, not having enough information about the practical results of psychoanalysis. Are we able through its application to obtain more thorough and more frequent results and in shorter time when all other psychotherapeutic measures fail? Is it the one form of psychotherapy which leads to happiness, and are there no cases where other methods are preferable? In order to answer these questions openly I will disillusion those who believe that the motto of the surgeon, *Cito, tuto et jucunde*, is applicable to analysis. Analysis is no quick but rather a very prolonged method of cure. Usually an analysis lasts for months, in severe cases, years. This can hardly be called a matter of convenience. It promises no absolute painlessness; in fact, tolerance of psychic pain which cannot be avoided and which has a real basis is one of the ends it hopes to develop in the patient. One will also permit himself no more than a surmise about the certainty of the final result. In no event does psychoanalysis belong to that group of enviable methods such as hypnotism which can simply blow symptoms away. It places no faith in the permanency of such methods; it is certain that the dust raised by such a process must settle somewhere. It rather seeks radically to clean the psychopathic foci. If anywhere, the proverb—*Si duo faciunt idem non est idem*—applies here. Psychoanalysis acknowledges that it is not suitable in all cases of neurosis; thus other forms of psychotherapy also have their field of application. At present it is not adapted to mass treatment. What it does anticipate in the future, however, is that the other methods will become permeated by its spirit. The trained analyst will have, as a hypnotist, a psychotherapist, or a director of an asylum, much better results and will show much better judgment than he who makes no effort to discover the probable etiology of the psychogenic symptoms from the data at hand. In this sense we can confidently prophesy that no form of psychotherapy will be able permanently to avoid being influenced by Freud's ideas. This actually takes place today to a large extent, even though the process is masked under a different standard.

The great changes which have taken place in psychiatry since Freud's concepts have penetrated the walls of asylums are well-known facts. No one is satisfied any longer with the traditional descriptive method of labeling cases according to their symptomatic grouping. There is a need for intelligible relationships and connections which certainly were not conspicuous in pre-Freudian literature. We can predict that the insane asylum will be transformed into a psychotherapeutic institution in which psychoanalytically trained physicians will occupy themselves with each case every day, and, if possible, for an hour a day. No matter how difficult it is to attain this ideal, it will hardly be possible to shun it. What the old master of French psychiatry,

Pinel, following the goodness of his heart, accomplished externally—releasing the psychopath from unnecessary fetters—Freud has repeated from the intellectual side. Due to his discovery, the symptoms of the insane have ceased to be a collection of abnormalities which by the unthinking were declared to be crazy, ridiculous, and without meaning. The psychopath also speaks a language which is intelligible to the competent expert. Thus the deep chasm which existed between the mentally normal and mentally deranged person was first bridged over.

The great transformation in the study of the neuroses and in psychiatry which Freud not only inaugurated but brought to a kind of completion in more than thirty years of indefatigable work is to be compared to the transformation in internal medicine through the clinical methods of percussion, auscultation, measurement of temperature, X-ray, bacteriology, and chemistry. Before these discoveries there were sensitive, successful physicians, too. But today no physician of normal mind would depend exclusively on his keen sense and purposely fail to convince himself objectively of the correctness or incorrectness of his reflections. Psychoanalysis has raised knowledge about the neuroses and psychoses to a new scientific level, and this work cannot be undone any more. Of course there are many ways by which medicine can make use of the Freudian ideas. One would be that psychoanalysis, as a distinct science, would be further suppressed and repressed so that its fruitful ideas seep along all possible routes into all branches of science. In this way it would be plowed under as fertilizer, so that the moral and aesthetic sense of gentlemanly scholars would not be injured by its unappetizing aspects. Thus they would be permitted to enjoy in composure the beautiful blossoms nourished by it. But to consider this possibility seriously is unbelievable. It has been the good fortune of the discoverer of psychoanalysis to live long enough to establish his work firmly and to protect it from these numerous attempts at dissolution.

Freud was also able to complete sufficiently the neglected research into the hidden powers behind instinctual life, so that finally he could turn to the more obvious and acceptable function of consciousness. I refer to his beginning in scientific ego psychology, which finally contained, in substantial form, explanations of the higher psychic functions—intelligence, conscience, morality, idealism, etc. Such explanations were sorely needed by his contemporaries. Freud certainly did not occupy himself with the aberrations of sexual life and with the animal aggressive instincts because of a personal preference, but because there was no other Hercules to bring order into this Augean stable. He was a plain investigator of reality; social views and prejudices occupied him little. Yet from the very beginning he recognized that, besides instinctual life, the power of repressing forces, social adjustment, and sublimation of these instincts were factors of equal if not greater importance in his studies. Overlooking this point can be attributed only to the blind hate or blind fear of his contemporaries. The result, however, was that one said he delved into the dirty instincts; the others hurled such expressions as "pansexuality" and "dangerous psychic epidemic" at his teachings.

But the period of these reactions of fury seems to be nearing its end. Even though they speak timidly, more and more voices, among them distinguished ones, at least partially confirm Freud's teachings. It is striking that such substantiations come not only from psychiatrists, but from circles of internists, gynecologists, pediatricians, dermatologists, and so on. They state that many a problematic case in their field of specialization has become intelligible and accessible to therapy only because of a psychoanalytic explanation. Consideration of unconscious psychic factors in the pathogenesis of disease seems to spread almost like an epidemic. Many distinguished physicians occupy themselves intensively with analytic therapy in organic disease. To be sure, these are only promising beginnings but their future significance cannot be denied. To medicine which has been segmented into all the specialities, psychoanalysis has been a benefactor, for it reminds one, in every form of disease, to treat the patient as well as the disease. This has always been recognized in principle, but rarely in practice because of the want of real psychologic knowledge. To use gross exaggeration, we could say that heretofore medicine has acted as though a patient were anencephalous and as though the highest comprehending powers, which we call psychic, had nothing to say in the matter of the struggles of the organs against the disease. It is certainly time that we take seriously the expression "the individual treatment of the patient."

The separatist movements which are manifest in all great ideas did not leave psychoanalysis untouched. But it is out of place to go into them in detail here. Suffice it to say that the importance of the individual schismatics is small compared to Freud's. It is unfair to mention their names along with his, as so many scientific publications often do. The whole incident reminds one of the satiric words of that thoughtful and original professor of pathology in Vienna, Samuel Stricker, who supplemented the communications of his own discoveries with the remark: "But then Mr. Modifier has to be considered." This does not imply that their efforts contain nothing of value or interest.

All institutes solely devoted to psychoanalysis owe their establishment to private initiative. Occasionally they have had to combat the indifference, even the antipathy, of official groups. Everywhere the universities have been the most conservative in their attitude. Nothing illustrates this better than the fact that the author of psychoanalysis has never been approached to give an official course of study, though he has been given the honorary title of professor for his accomplishments.

It was a divine inspiration which prompted Freud to introduce his *Interpretation of Dreams* with the prophetic phrase, *Flectere si nequeo superos, acheronta movebo*. With this he meant to characterize the scientific fact that the most important problems of the human mind are attacked only from the depths of the unconscious. But the motto may be interpreted in another sense.

I can state that until Freud, medicine had been taught as a purely natural science. One attended a health technical high school from which one graduated with much theoretical and practical knowledge, yet ignorant of the human psyche. But out in the world of medical practice the psychological factor in therapy is as important as the objective finding in the organ. I can imagine how much effort and pain might have been spared had I, as a student, been taught the art of dealing with transference and resistance. I envy the medical student of the near future who will be taught this. The humanization of the university course of study will become an absolute necessity and it finally will come about.

A particular difficulty in learning psychoanalysis lies in the fact that its method, as mentioned, is dualistic or ultraquistic. Accurate observation of the objective attitude of the patient, including what he says, that is the so-called "behavior," is not enough. Psychoanalysis demands of the physician untiring sensitivity to all of the patient's ideational associations, his emotions, and his unconscious processes. To do this it is necessary that the physician have a flexible, plastic psyche himself. He can attain this only by being analyzed himself. How the future medical student will attain this profound self-knowledge is a difficult question to answer. The training of a psychoanalytic specialist requires, apart from theoretical study, a didactic analysis of at least a year's duration. One cannot demand as much of the practitioner of the future, yet this sometimes painful process cannot be dispensed with altogether. It is an old, well-known fact that diabetic physicians are most sensitive to the handling of diabetic patients, and the same is true of the tuberculous physician. The Viennese professor Oser who lectured on gastric pathology told us that he was interested in the subject because of his own stomach disorder. Naturally we cannot expect the future physician to expose himself to and contract all sorts of infectious diseases in order better to understand and treat patients with such disease. Yet psychoanalysis demands something of this kind when it requires a psychic sensitivity on the part of the physician to the abnormalities of the patient. The difference between this situation and the one just mentioned, however, lies in the fact that each of us, has, according to the discoveries of psychoanalysis, virtual potentiality for his sympathetic feeling in his own unconscious. We need only remove the acquired resistance to this unconscious power to make it conscious, so that it becomes serviceable in the understanding of the patient. I am convinced that efforts in such directions are more than worth while. Scientifically founded knowledge of mankind will help bring back to the practical physician the authority which he has lost as adviser to the individual, to his family, and to society when they find themselves in difficult situations. I trust it will be remembered whose lifework was dedicated to raising his position and authority again.

A few more words about the geographical extension of psychoanalysis, or as the man Hoche called it—the psychoanalytic plague. Completely misunderstanding the essentials of psychoanalysis, some particularly vicious antagonists of Freud stated that psychoanalysis, or as they termed it, sexual psychoanalysis, could have been produced only in the frivolous, gay atmosphere of Vienna. One comment from an Anglo-Saxon country was, "Perhaps one dreams such things in Austria's capital city, but our dreams are more respectable." Psychoanalysis claims that repression of libidinal tendencies is the cause of neuroses. Hence, according to Freud's opponents, such a teaching must have arisen in a land where prudery and repression are at home. But in reality a country not characterized particularly by prudery was the most unsuitable place for the recognition of psychoanalysis. France, Austria, and Italy are such countries where psychoanalysis met with the greatest opposition, while England and America, countries with a particularly rigid sex morality, showed themselves much more receptive.

Some did not miss the opportunity to judge Freud's work from a racial angle and to attribute it to his Semitic blood. It is said that Lord Balfour, in the dedication of the new university of Jerusalem, called Freud one of the representatives of intellectual Judaism. But many others referred to his Semitism with much less goodwill. I do not believe that our knowledge of racial psychology has developed to a point where we can say something definite about the soundness of these remarks. At any rate, these comments are rather an honor to the Jewish race than a debasement of Freud.

In conclusion, I wish to point out that Freud tore down the rigid line of demarcation between natural and mental science. Psychoanalysis has not only promoted mutual understanding between the physician and the patient, but it has also made natural and mental science understandable to each other whereas before they were strange and foreign. To attain such an end Freud had to renounce his feeling of self-complacency which has characterized the physician of the past. He began to believe, in the saying of Schweniger, that "every person must be a physician and every physician must be a person."

Freud's influence on medicine signifies a formal mutation, a radical stimulus to the development of this science. Potentiality for such development might have existed for a long time, yet for actual execution it had to await the coming of a personality like Freud.

This paper was originally published as "Freuds Einfluss auf die Medizin" in *Bausteine zür Psychoanalyse* (Leipzig: Internationaler psychoanalytischer Verlag, 1927). In 1933, it was published in the *International Journal of Psycho-Analysis*, Vol. II, 1933; in *Psychoanalytische Bewegung*, Vol. V, 1933; and in *Psychoanalysis Today*, edited by Sandor Lorand (New York: Covici-Friede, 1933). In 1955, it appeared in *Final Contributions to the Problems and Methods of Psychoanalysis*, edited by Michael Balint (New York: Basic Books, 1955). The translator is unknown.

Sándor Ferenczi belonged to Freud's closest and most intimate group of followers. In 1909, he accompanied Freud on his visit to Clark University, in Worcester, Massachusetts, and also visited this country several times on lecture tours. He analyzed some of the foremost American psychoanalysts and had a considerable influence on people like Clara Thompson and Erich Fromm.

The origin and structure of the superego

Ernest Jones

It is desirable to state clearly at the outset that this paper is of a peculiarly tentative character. The special occasion for which it was written, and the exigency of a time limit, induced me to attack an intricate theme when my own opinions about it are the very reverse of mature. Indeed, the essential object of the present contribution is merely to define a little more closely some of the complex problems involved and to invite further discussion of them; I would attach only a very restricted validity to any positive suggestions that may emerge in the course of the present remarks. The subject itself is concerned with one of the most important contributions that Freud has made to the science of psychoanalysis he created, and the spectacle of the following attempt to apprehend his latest teachings will serve as well as any other to illustrate the ever pioneering nature of Freud's work and the fact that his mind remains the youngest and freshest of any among us.

The particular problem to be considered here is that of the origin and actual structure of the superego, that is, the nature and genesis of the various trends composing it. As Freud himself says, "In other matters—for instance, concerning the origin and function of the superego—a good deal remains insufficiently elucidated."[1]

As to the validity and value of the conception itself there will be universal agreement, for the reasons Freud gave when he postulated it can be definitely confirmed in any character analysis, and perhaps in any properly completed analysis. Further, a number of formulations in regard to it would appear to be equally well established. Thus, the genesis of the superego is certainly connected with the passing of the Œdipus complex, and the nuclear and essential part of its composition may be regarded as the direct imprint made on the personality by the conflicts relating to this complex;[2] Freud neatly designates it as the heir of the Œdipus complex.[3] Much is known also about the relation of the superego to the outer world and to the other institutions of the mind. The function it exercises is perhaps its clearest feature. It is to criticize the ego and to cause pain to the latter whenever it tends to accept impulses proceeding from the repressed part of the id. In this connection we may note the improvement Freud has effected in the terminology relating to the idea of guilt. He would confine the expression "consciousness of guilt," or "sense of guilt," to the perception of guilt on the part of consciousness[4] and substitute that of "need for punishment" (Strafbedürfnis) when it concerns the unconscious ego, reserving "criticism" for the operation performed by the superego. The relation of both these active and passive aspects of the phenomenon to consciousness, however, is a very variable one; either or

[1] Sigmund Freud, Collected Papers (New York: Basic Books, 1959), II, 250.
[2] Sigmund Freud, The Ego and the Id (New York: W. W. Norton, 1962), pp. 18–29.
[3] Ibid., p. 28.
[4] Ibid., p. 39.

both may be unconscious, the latter more often than the former.[5]

When, however, we leave these valuable broad generalizations and come to a closer study of the problems involved, a considerable number of awkward questions present themselves. To mention only a few at this point: How can we conceive of the same institution as being both an object that presents itself to the id to be loved instead of the parents[6] and as an active force criticizing the ego? If the superego arises from incorporating the abandoned love object,[7] how comes it that in fact it is more often derived from the parent of the same sex? If it is composed of elements taken from the "moral" non-sexual ego instincts, as we should expect from the part it plays in the repression of the sexual incestuous ones, whence does it derive its sadistic, i.e. sexual, nature? These and many other apparent contradictions need to be resolved. Finally, there is every reason to think that the concept of the superego is a nodal point where we may expect all the obscure problems of Œdipus complex and narcissism on the one hand, and hate and sadism on the other, to meet.

Before taking up the problems concerning the origin and structure of the superego, it is necessary to say something about its general relations, particularly the topographical ones.

Relation to the outer world, the ego and the id.—The ego is the part of the id that is altered by the influence of the outer world, and the superego is a differentiated part of the ego,[8] again one brought about under the influence of

---

[5] *Collected Papers*, II, 266.
[6] *The Ego and the Id*, p. 11.
[7] *Ibid.*, p. 9 ff.
[8] *Ibid.*, pp. 8–9.

the outer world. On the one hand we read[9] that the superego stands nearer to the id than does the ego, is independent
of the latter and represents to it the demands of the id,
though the id can also influence the ego directly as well as
through the superego.[10] On the other hand it is just through
its connection with the outer world, the reality demands
of which it represents, that the superego gains its power of
affecting the ego.[11] The full explanation seems to be that
the superego in some obscure way combines influences from
both the inner and the outer world, from the id and from
external reality, and that these are then directed toward
the ego.[12]

Relation to Consciousness.—Two statements of Freud's
bear on this point. The superego may be for the greater
part unconscious and inaccessible to the ego.[13] It dips deeply
into the id and is therefore farther removed from consciousness than is the ego.[14] It is probable that the superego may
be partly conscious, partly preconscious and partly unconscious; further, that its relation to consciousness varies at
different times. That it should be as a rule less conscious
than is the ego may be explained by its relation to outer
reality, for this relation was far closer in the past (in infancy) than it is in the present.

Relation to Repression.—It is the ego, not the superego,
that performs the act of repression, though it commonly
does so in obedience to the demands of the latter.[15] It is
important, however, to note that, especially in hysteria, the
ego can keep from consciousness, i.e. repress, the feeling of

---

[9] *Ibid.*, pp. 23, 28, 29.
[10] *Ibid.*, p. 35.
[11] *Collected Papers*, II, 151, 153.
[12] *Ibid.*, pp. 253, 264.
[13] *The Ego and the Id*, p. 20.
[14] *Ibid.*, p. 28.
[15] *Ibid.*, p. 29.

guilt provoked by the superego's attack on it.[16] It should be possible in the future to describe this in economic terms as a balance between different amounts of pleasure and pain.

Relation to External Love Object.—Freud writes:[17] "If a sexual object has to be given up, there is not infrequently brought about in its place the change in the ego which one must describe, for instance in melancholia, as an erecting of the object within the ego," and he adds "the nearer closer conditions of this replacement are not yet known to us." Throughout he appears to assume that the superego, which we know to be the heir of the Œdipus complex, results in this way from the incorporating of the parental figure that had to be given up in its sexual connection. But the evidence is fairly extensive that, though the superego may be derived from either parent and is commonly enough derived from both, it is normally and predominantly derived, not from the love object that has been abandoned, but from the parent of the same sex. With the boy, for instance, it is derived in the main from the father, and when it is derived from the mother the chances are great that he will be homosexual. Freud himself points out this paradox,[18] but offers no explanation of it. The discussion of bisexuality that follows in the context doubtless explains the facts of there being two types and of their often being mixed, but it in no way accounts for the phenomenon of the more normal type in which the heterosexual person derives his superego from the parent of the same sex as himself. It would therefore seem that a necessary condition for the process of incorporation is that the object incorporated must have thwarted the love impulses of the subject.

If this reasoning is sound, then it can only be that the

---

[16] *Loc. cit.*

[17] *Op. cit.*, p. 19.

[18] *Ibid.*, p. 16.

mechanism of superego formation normally follows the order which Freud has described in connection with the attitude of a homosexual toward his brothers,[19] namely, that original rivalry of a hostile kind was replaced by a friendly object choice, which in its turn was replaced by identification. Applying this to the Œdipus situation, and taking again the case of the boy, we must assume that the superego usually arises from identification with the father where the initial hostile rivalry had been replaced by homosexual love. In the less usual and less normal case, that of the homosexual man, there are two possibilities open. Either the same mechanism as that just suggested holds good, which means that, the feminine component of his bisexuality being predominant, he deals with his jealous rivalry of his mother by a passing object love followed by identification with her, or else the identification is a means of dealing with hatred proceeding from the fact, characteristic of this type, that his castration fears are more closely connected with the mother than with the father. Both explanations accord with the law that the superego is derived from a thwarting object. The two explanations differ in that with the first congenital sexuality would be the ultimate cause of the undue reaction to the mother, with the second this might or might not be so.

It will be seen that here stress is laid on *hostility*[20] being the essential condition of superego formation. This one may relate to the predominantly sadistic nature of the later superego, a matter which will be discussed presently. To recapitulate for the sake of clearness: it is suggested that

---

[19] *Ibid.*, p. 18.

[20] Cf. Freud's remarks on ambivalence in connection with melancholic identification. *Collected Papers*, (New York: Basic Books 1959), IV, 161.

the superego is derived from the thwarting parent, irrespective of whether this happens to be the primary love object or not; normally it is a secondary love object, the parent of the same sex.

The replacement of object cathexis by identification brings about a profound change in the libidinal situation. The image thus incorporated into the (super) ego serves itself as an object to the libidinal impulses proceeding from the id, so that more of them are directed toward the ego as a whole than previously; this constitutes what Freud terms "secondary narcissism."[21] Along with this goes a desexualization of the impulses, a kind of sublimation, and this important process gives rise to interesting problems. Freud hints that it is due to the giving up of sexual aims implied in the change from allo-erotic into narcissistic libido. To quote his exact words: "The transformation of object libido into narcissistic libido that takes place here evidently brings with it a giving up of sexual aims, a desexualization, i.e. a kind of sublimation."[22] But narcissistic libido is still sexual as is even an impulse inhibited in its aim (affection), and both in moral masochism and in the obsessional neurosis we see that the impulses concerned with the superego need not be desexualized; it is plain, further, that there are all degrees of desexualization. So that there must be some further factors at work to account for this interesting change when it occurs.

Two further clues are provided elsewhere by Freud. In the first place he points out that the superego is not simply a residuum of the object choices, but also signifies an energetic reaction formation against them. "Its relation to the ego is not all comprehended in the exhortation 'You

---

[21] *The Ego and the Id*, p. 9.
[22] *Loc. cit.*

ought to be like the father'; it also includes the prohibition 'You may not be like the father' i.e., you may not do everything he does; many things are his prerogative."[23] In other words, the superego consists in the incorporation only of the "moral," thwarting, and asexual elements of the object. The allo-erotic libido of the subject's id somehow accomplishes the extraordinary feat of substituting this loveless image for the previous love object; by some magic he manages to love with all the strength of his being just that which he had most reason to hate and fear. It is very possible, however, that from the wreckage of his own desires he is able by means of the identification with the father to save at least in a vicarious way the object relation which the latter bears to the mother; if so, this vicarious gratification would have to be much deeper in the unconscious than the superego.

A second and more valuable clue is afforded by the following considerations. If we inquire into the actual composition of the superego, the most obvious constituent to be perceived is sadism,[24] usually desexualized. It is presumably to be accounted for as a pre-genital regression of the libido that is no longer allowed to be directed toward the love object; we know that regression is a common sequel to frustration. But this is only the result of a reaction on the part of the endangered ego, which yields to the (castration) threat to its integrity and defends itself by repression of the incestuous impulses. This threat to the primary narcissism must also mobilize the non-sexual ego instincts, notably

---

[23] *Op. cit.*, p. 14.

[24] The finding is not surprising when one reflects how sadistic and persecutory even ordinary (outwardly directed) morality often is; in the formation of the superego we have an example of the "turning round upon the subject," which Freud described in connection with sadism as one of the vicissitudes of instincts (*Collected Papers*, IV, 70). Cf. *The Ego and the Id*, p. 43.

hate and fear, and probably all those which I have grouped under the name of "repulsion instincts."[25] The problem that here arises is the relation of the two groups of instincts to each other—roughly speaking, of the hate group[26] to the love group. In *The Ego and the Id*[27] Freud supposes that any previous connection between the two undergoes a process of "de-fusion." He takes for granted the desexualization of the libidinal impulses as a necessary consequence of the secondary narcissism and suggests that as the result of this desexualization the libido loses its power to bind the aggressive tendencies, which are therefore set free; hence the cruelty of the superego. To me at least an alternative hypothesis which he had previously put forward in the *Triebe und Triebschicksale* essay[28] appeals as more likely. In speaking of ambivalence he shows illuminatingly how the ego instincts and sexual instincts mutually influence each other, and how they can form a unity during the pre-genital phases of libidinal organization. "When the sexual function is governed by the ego instincts, as at the stage of the sadistic-anal organization, they impart the qualities of hate to the instinct's aim as well. . . . This admixture of hate in love is to be traced in part to those preliminary stages of love which have not been wholly outgrown, and in part is based upon reactions of aversion and repudiation on the part of the ego instincts. . . . In both cases, therefore, the admixture of hate may be traced to the source of the self-preservation instincts. When a love relationship with a given object is broken off, it is not infrequently succeeded by hate, so that we receive the impression of a transforma-

---

[25] Transcription of the meeting of the Seventh International Congress of Psychology, 1924, p. 231.
[26] Freud's "death instinct." I find myself unable to operate with this philosophical concept in a purely clinical discussion.
[27] *The Ego and the Id*, p. 43.
[28] *Collected Papers*, IV, 82.

tion of love into hate. This descriptive characterization is amplified by the view that, when this happens, the hate which is motivated by considerations of reality is reinforced by a regression of the love to the sadistic preliminary stage, so that the hate acquires an erotic character and the continuity of a love relation is ensured." One may ask whether this does not describe the changes that occur when the superego is formed. That would mean a fusion, rather than a de-fusion, of the two groups. And it may be that the secret of the desexualization of the libidinal impulses, perhaps also the preceding regression of them to the anal-sadistic level, may be found in the influence on them of the hate impulses (ego instinct in general). Whether this holds good for the desexualization and sublimation which Freud[29] suggests occurs at every identification is, of course, another matter. On the other side the libido would give an erotic coloring to the ego impulses, so that the hate would come to partake of the quality of sadism and fuse with the sadism resulting from libidinal regression.

We may now attempt to describe schematically the changes that ensue on the passing of the Œdipus complex and the replacement of it by the superego.

A. *Ego Instincts.*—These "reactive" instincts are all stimulated by the unfriendly situation in the outer world (parents) that leads to the repression of the incestuous wishes. The hatred for the rival, the half of the Œdipus complex which is presently to be resolved by homosexual identification, arises later in time than these wishes.

Fear. The fear of castration constitutes the kernel of the dread which the ego displays in regard to the superego,[30] and this is evidently a displacement from the father. It is

---

[29] *Collected Papers*, II, 273.
[30] *The Ego and the Id*, p. 44.

continued later as a sensitiveness to conscience, that is, as a sense of guilt.[31]

Hate. This is activated against whichever parent is felt to be the obstacle to the love impulses, whether that be the main love object or not.

1. Part is repressed, but continues to be directed against the external object or subsequent substitutes for this.
2. Part fuses with the libidinal impulses and helps to give them their sadistic character. This part operates from the id via the superego and is directed against the actual ego whenever this tends to admit repressed libidinal or hate impulses of such a kind as to bring the risk of re-arousing the external disapproval and danger. This "turning round upon the subject" of impulses previously directed against the parent is a defensive procedure designed to avert the wrath of the parent; it is akin to the mechanism of the self-imposed penance among religious people.

B. *Sexual Instincts.*—As was indicated above, the ego defends itself against external danger by repressing the genital impulses directed toward the love object. Regression to the anal-sadistic level ensues, but the relation of this process to the frustration and to the influence of the ego instincts is not clear. The libido is then redistributed as follows:[32]

1. A part continues to be directed to the parents, both heterosexually and homosexually, but as a form of libido "inhibited in its aim." This is the ordinary affection felt by the child for its parents. It is apt

---

[31] *Loc. Cit.*
[32] It is doubtful if one can apply the term desexualization to the first two of these four groups.

to be weakened whenever the parent's conduct falls below the standard set by the superego, i.e., whenever the identification of parent and superego is impaired. Where the affection consciously felt for the parent of the opposite sex is excessive one may suspect excessive identification with that parent, with subsequent homosexual subject inversion (in Ferenczi's sense).

2. A part becomes secondary narcissism. This is another way in which the allo-erotic impulses can achieve indirect gratification, for the superego toward which they are here directed is in great part a substitute for the parent. In the case where this parent is of the same sex, which is the most frequent one, a previous deflection has taken place from heterosexuality toward homosexuality.

3. A part regresses and fuses with the hate instincts to constitute sadism. To begin with this is probably also directed from the id toward the superego, as a substitute for the hated parent, but it passes through the superego and is applied (apparently by it) to the ego itself. It operates in the way mentioned above in connection with hate. This part of the libido is normally desexualized, but the change varies greatly in completeness.

4. It is probable that other active components of the libido follow the same course as the last group. Thus in the attitude of the superego toward the ego, particularly in regard to such matters as duty, order, and the like, it is hard not to see traces of the anal component of the anal-sadistic phase. Similarly scopophilic elements may perhaps be concerned in the careful "watching" exercised over the ego.

We thus see that the superego arises as a compromise between the desire to love and the desire to be loved. On the one hand it provides an object for the libidinal impulses of the id when the external object is no longer available, whereas on the other hand it represents the renouncing of incest which is the only condition under which the parents' approval (i.e., affection) can be retained.

This paper was originally read before the British Psycho-Analytical Society on March 3, 1926. It was subsequently published in the *International Journal of Psycho-Analysis*, Vol. VII, 1926, and in the *International Zeitschrift für Psychoanalyse*, Vol. XII, 1926. It later appeared in *Papers on Psychoanalysis*, by Ernest Jones (5th ed.; New York: William Wood, 1948).

Ernest Jones was Freud's Boswell. He became, during Freud's life, his foremost interpreter and protector. His monumental biography of Freud, published between 1953 and 1957, is a landmark in the history of psycho-analysis and the psychoanalytic movement.

The necessity of metaphysics

James J. Putnam

Some years ago, at the Weimar Congress of the International Psycho-Analytic Association, I read a paper on the importance of a knowledge of philosophy and metaphysics for psychoanalysts regarded as students of human life. Perhaps if I had had the experience and ability to contribute the results of some original analytic investigation on specific lines, I should not then have ventured into the philosophic field. Perhaps, indeed, if those conditions now obtained I should not be bringing forward similar arguments again, and if anyone feels tempted to maintain that philosophic speculation is a camp of refuge for those who, in consequence of temperamental limitations and infantile fixations which ought to be overcome, draw back from the more robust study of emotional repressions on scientific lines, I should admit that the allegation contains an element of truth. But in spite of this, and in spite of the fact that there is some truth also in the statement that the effects—good and bad—of emotional repression make themselves felt, as a partial influence, in all the highest reaches of human endeavor, including art, literature, and religion;—in spite of these partial truths, philosophy and metaphysics are the only means through which the essential nature of many tendencies can be studied of which psychoanalysis describes only the transformations. And this being so it is perhaps reasonable that one paper should be read at an annual meeting such as this, where men assemble whose duty it is to study the human mind in all its aspects.

I presume that just as, and just because, men have minds *and* bodies, an evolutionary history in the ordinary sense and a mental history in a sense not commonly considered, so there will always be two, or perhaps three, parties among psychologists and men of science, and each one, in so far as it is limited in its vision, may be considered as abnormal, if one will. I decline, however, to admit that the temperamental peculiarities of one group are more in need either of justification or of rectification through psychoanalysis than those of the others. It is probably true that emotional tension often plays a larger part among persons who love a priori reasoning—the "tender-minded" of Dr. James—than it does in those who work through observation; but on the other hand exclusively empirical attitude has its limitations and its dangers. Philosophy and metaphysics deal more distinctively with essential function—that is, with real existence—while natural science and the genetic psychology (of which psychoanalysis, strictly speaking, is a branch) deal rather with appearances and with structure. Both are in need of investigation. The *form* which art, religion, and literature assume is determined by men's personal experiences and special cravings. The *essential motive* of art and religion is, however, the dim recognition by men of their relation to the creative spirit of the universe.

No one can doubt that function logically precedes structure; or if anyone does doubt this, he need only observe his own experience and see how in every new acquisition of knowledge or of power there come, first, the thought, the idea, then the effort, next the habit, and finally the modification of cerebral mechanism, in which the effort and the habit become represented in relatively permanent and static form. In fact, the crux of the whole discussion between science and metaphysics turns on, or harks back to the discussion between function and structure; and it is the latter, in the sense in which I mean the word, that has had of late a too large share of our attention.

The enterprise on which we are all of us embarked—whether we define it as an investigation, pure and simple, into human nature and human motives, or as a therapeutic attempt to relieve invalids of their symptoms—is a larger one than it is commonly conceived of as being. Each physician and each investigator has, indeed, the right to say that for practical reasons he prefers to confine his attention to some single portions of one or the other of these tasks, be it never so small. But each one should regard himself as virtually under an obligation to recognize the respects in which this chosen task is incomplete. Every physicist is aware that there is some form of energy underlying, or rather expressing itself in, light and heat and gravitation. Physicists do not study this form of energy, not because they do not wish to but simply because they cannot do so by the only methods that they are allowed to use. But, as a reaction of defense, they sometimes assert that no one else can do so either, that this underlying energy cannot be explained. To say this is, however, in my judgment, to misappreciate what an explanation is.

To explain any matter is to discover the points of similarity, or virtual identity, between the matter studied and ourselves. But in order to do this thoroughly, or rather in order to do it with relation to the essential nature of some form of energy (the "libido," for example, considered as an unpicturable force) one must first consider what we, the investigators, are, not at our less good, but at our best. It is with us, as given, with our best qualities regarded as defining in part the Q. E. D. of the experiment, that the investigation must begin. The nature of any and every form of real underlying energy or essence must be defined in terms of our sense of our own will and freedom. And this means that we must conceive and describe ourselves, and expect to conceive and to describe the powers that animate us, no longer as a system of forces subject to the so-called laws of nature (which are, in reality, not immutable) but as relatively free, creative agents; no longer as the product of the interplay of instincts, but as individuals possessed of real reason, real power of love and real self-consistent will. To claim to study the effects of the "libido," to which we ascribe the vast powers with which we are familiar, yet fail to seek in it what would correspond to our own best attributes, would be to lay aside our duties as students of human nature. It would be to confine our attention to the "structure" of the mind, the form under which it manifests itself, without having studied the laws of its action under conditions which are more favorable to its development.

It must, now, have struck students of psychoanalytic literature that a marked tendency has been shown toward supplementing the study of structure—that is, the detailed history of men's experiences and evolution, regarded as sequences of phenomena—by the study of the function or creative energy for which the experiences stand. Silberer, whose work is endorsed by Freud, has gone to a considerable length in this direction; and the whole tendency of Freud's insistence on the relevancy, in the mental sphere,

of the law of the conservation of energy has been a movement, though, I think, a narrow one, in this direction. More
recently, Jung has emphasized the importance of this tendency, and has dwelt more strongly, as I think, than the facts
warrant, on the supposed unwillingness of Freud to recognize its importance.

Behind the experiences of childhood, for example, lie the
temperamental trends of childhood, and it is these with
which we really need to get acquainted; for these trends,
if not the whole causes and equivalents of the experiences
which are recounted to us by our patients, constitute the
conditions without which the latter would not have been
what they became.

But Jung himself, strangely enough, in both of his carefully prepared arguments, specifically rejects all intention
of dealing "metaphysically" with this theme, in spite of the
fact that every movement toward a fuller recognition of
creative energy is nothing less than metaphysics, even
though not in name.

The skilled observer, scrutinizing the motives and peer-
ing into the history of the person whose traits and trends he
is called on to investigate, must see, in imagination, not only
a vast host of acts, but also a vast network of intersecting
lines of energy of which the casual observer, and even the
intimate friend, may be wholly unaware. We call these
lines of energy by many special names,—"libido" or "Ur-
libido," first of all, then love and hate and jealousy, and
so on.

What are these lines of energy, and how can we study
them to the best purpose? Obviously they are incomplete
editions of the love and reason and will, the laws of which
we can study to best advantage in ourselves and in men
where they are displayed in their best, that is, in their most

constructive form. To make such studies is to recognize metaphysics, but instead of doing this tacitly and implicitly we should do it openly and explicitly.

The study of human nature should, in short, begin at the top, rather than at the bottom; just as, if one had to choose what phase of a symphony one would choose in order to get an idea of its perfection, one would take some culminating moment rather than the first few notes simply because they were the first. To be accurate, one could not do justice to the symphony except by studying it as a whole, and similarly one should study the man as a whole, including his relations to the universe as a whole. It is as wholes that great poets conceived of their poems and great artists of their pictures, and it is as a whole that each and every human life, standing as it does as the representative of the *body* of the universe, and the *spirit* of the universe, on the other, should implicitly be viewed.

The psychologist should sympathize deeply with the anatomist and the physiologist and the student of cerebral pathology, but equally deeply with the philosopher and the metaphysician who study the implications, present although hidden, that point to the bonds between the individual and the universe. To fail to recognize that these bonds exist—as is done when the attempt is made to study human beings as if they were really and exclusively the product of their historic past conceived of in an organic sense—would be to try to build one half of an arch and expect it to endure. The truth is, we do not, in my opinion, genuinely believe that a human is nothing but the product of his organic past, or the product of his experience.

We believe, by implication, in our metaphysical selves and our corresponding obligations, more strongly than we have taught ourselves to recognize. But to this fact we make ourselves blind through a species of repression, just as many a child, confident of its parents' affection, assumes, for his own temporary purposes, the right to accuse them of hostile intentions which they do not entertain.

We forget, or repress, the fact that the mind of man cannot be made subject to the laws of physics, and yet we proceed to deal with the phenomena dependent on the working of the mind of man as if these laws actually did prevail.

The misleading effects of this tendency are clearly seen where it is a question of the conclusions to be drawn from the researches admirable in themselves, made under the influence of the genetic method.

The notion seems to prevail that we should prepare ourselves for the formation of just ideas with regard to the mode in which the higher faculties of men come into existence by wiping the slate clean to the extent of assuming that we have before us no data except some few acts or thoughts that are definable in the simplest possible terms, and then watching what happens as the situation becomes more complicated. But one is apt to forget, in doing this, that there is one thing which we cannot wipe off the slate —namely, ourselves, not taken in the Bergsonian sense alone, but as fully-fledged persons, possessed of the very qualities for which we undertake to search, yet without the possession of which the search could not begin. This does not, of course, militate against the value of these genetic researches in one sense. The study of evolutional sequences is still, and forever will be, of enormous value. But it does not teach us nearly as much of the nature of real creativeness as we can learn through the introspection of ourselves in the fullest sense; and I maintain that psychoanalysts are persons who could do this to advantage.

Is not the notion that through the careful watching of the sequences of the evolutionary process, as if from without, we can get an adequate idea of the forces that really are at work, exactly the delusion by which the skillful juggler tries to deceive his audience when he directs their attention to the shifting objects that he manipulates, and away from his own swiftly moving hands?

My contention is that there are other means of studying the force which we call "libido" besides that of noting its effects. The justification for this statement is that the force itself is identical, in the last analysis, with that which we feel within ourselves and know as reason, as imagination, and as will, conscious of themselves, and capable of giving to us, directly or indirectly, the only evidence we could ever hope to get, for the existence of real creativeness, spontaneity and freedom.

Every work of art, worthy of the name, gives evidence of the action not alone of a part of a man, but of the whole man; not only of his repressed emotions, but of his intelligence and insight, and of relationships existing between his life and all the other forms of life with which his own is interwoven.

Unity must prevail throughout all nature. Either we are —altogether, and through and through, our best as well as our less good—nothing but the expressions of repressed cravings, in the sense that they or the conflicts based on them constitute the final *causa vera* of all progress; or else the best that is in us and also our repressed cravings are alike due to the action of a form of energy which is virtually greater than either one of them, inasmuch as it has the capacity of developing into something greater than either.

This is the agency which we should pre-eminently study, and it is best studied under conditions when instead of being obviously subject to repression, it is most free from repression. That is, it is best studied as it appears in the thoughts and conduct of the best men, at their best, their most constructive moments.

We cannot use our power of reason to deny our reason; for in so doing we affirm the very thing which we deny. Nor are we under the necessity of using our reason to affirm our reason, since that is the datum without which we cannot undertake our task.

If this view is sound, what practical conclusions can we draw from it? I wish to insist on this question because it was distinctly and positively with the practical end in mind that I ventured to write this paper, and I suggest the following as a few of these conclusions.

1. We should not speak of the "libido," in whatever sense this word is taken, as if it were a fixed quantity, like so much heat, or so much fluid, that is, as representing so much measurable force. One current notion which has played a very useful part in psychoanalytic work, yet is misleading in its tendency, is that the "libido" may be likened to a river which if it cannot find an outlet through its normal channel is bound to overflow its banks and perhaps furrow out a new path. This conception is based on this same law of the conservation of energy to which reference has been made. If, however, I am right in my contention that the "libido" is only one manifestation of an energy —greater than simply "vital"—which can be studied to the best purpose only among men whose powers have been cultivated to the best advantage, then it will be seen that this conception of "libido" as a force of definite amount is not justifiable by the facts.

One does not find that love or reason is subject to this quantitative law. On the contrary, the persons whom most of us recognize as of the highest type do not love any given individual less because their love takes in another. The bond of love holds not only three, but an indefinite number.

The same statement may be made with regard to reason and to will. The power and quantity of them are not exhausted but are increased by use.

I maintain, then, that although the "libido," in so far as it is regarded as an instinct, does not stand on the same footing with the reason and disinterested love of a person of high cultivation and large views, neither does it stand on the same footing with the physical energy that manifests itself in light and heat and gravitation.

When we come to deal with man and any of his attributes, or as we find them at any age, we ought to look upon him, in my estimation, as animated in some measure by his self-foreshadowing best. And whether it is dreams with which we have to do, or neurotic conflicts, or willfulness, or regression, we shall learn to see, more and more, as we become accustomed to look for evidences thereof, the signs of this sort of promise, just as we might hope to learn to find, more and more, through the inspection of a lot of seeds of different plants, the evidences which would enable us to see the different outcomes which each one is destined to achieve, even though, at first, they all looked just alike.

2. The next point has reference to "sublimation." This outcome of individual evolution, as defined by Freud, has a strictly social, not an ethical, meaning. Jung also, in the interesting paper referred to, in his description of the rational aims of psychoanalysis, makes sublimation (though he does not there use the word) the equivalent of a subjective sense of well-being, combined with the maximum of biologic effectiveness.

"Psychoanalysis should be a biological method, which will unite a very subjective individual experience with a most valuable biological effort."*

But in my opinion, while it may be true that the psycho-analyst may often have reason to be thankful if he can claim a therapeutic outcome of this sort, the logical goal of a psychoanalytic treatment is not covered by the securing of a relative freedom from subjective distress, even when combined with the satisfactory fulfillment of one's biologic mission. A man has higher destinies than this, and the sense of incompleteness felt by the neurotic patient, which was emphasized by Janet and is recognized by us all, must be more or less painfully felt by every man whose conscience does not assure him that he is really working for an end greater than that here specified. The logical end of a psy-choanalytic treatment is the recovery of a full sense of one's highest destiny and origin and of the bearings and mean-ings of one's life.

On similar grounds I think that the conflicts to which all men find themselves subjected, must be considered, in the last analysis, as conflicts of an ethical description. For it is only in ethical terms that one can define one's relation to the universe regarded as a whole, just as it is only in ethical terms that a man could describe his sense of obliga-tion to support the dignity of fine family traditions or the ideals represented by a team or a social group of which he felt reason to be proud. I realize that a man's sense of pride of his family, his team or his country may be a symptom of narcissistic self-adulation; but like all such signs and symbols—the symbol of the church tower, for example—this is a case where two opposing meanings meet. Every act and motive of our lives, from infancy to age, is con-

* *Editor's Tr.*

trolled by two sets of influences, the general nature of which has here been made sufficiently clear. They correspond on the one hand, to the numerous partial motives which psychoanalysis studies to great advantage, and on the other hand, to the ethical motives which are only thoroughly studied by philosophy.

3. Another conclusion, which seems to me practically of great importance, follows from this same view. Everyone who has studied carefully the life histories of patients, especially of children, and has endeavored in so doing to follow step by step the experiences through which they reach the various milestones on their journey, must have been astonished to observe the evidences of *preparedness* on their part for each new step in this long journey. Human beings seem predestined, as it were, not only in a physical but in a mental sense, for what is coming, and the indications of this in the mental field are greater than the conditions of organic evolution could readily account for. The transcendency of the mind over the brain shows itself here as elsewhere.

We are told that our visions of the unpicturable, the ideal world, which our imagination paints and which our logical reasoning calls for as the necessary cap or final corollary to any finite world which our intelligence can actually define—that such visions are nothing but the pictures of infantile desires projected on to a great screen and made to mock us with the appearance of reality.

I have nothing whatever to say against the value of the evidence that a portion of our visions are of this origin. In fact, I believe this as heartily as does anyone. But I desire strenuously to oppose the view tacitly implied in the statement of the projection theory just cited, the acceptance of which as an exclusive doctrine would involve the virtual rejection of our right, as scientific men, to rely on the principle that the evidence afforded by logical presuppositions and logical inference is as cogent as that furnished through observation.

It is, in my opinion, just because we all belong to a world which is in outline not "in the making" but completed—because, in short, we are in one sense like heirs returning to our estates—that this remarkable preparedness of each child is found that impresses us so strongly. The universe is, in a sense, ours by prescriptive right and by virtue of the constitution of our minds. *But the unity of such a universe must, of course, be of a sort that includes and indeed implies diversity and conflict as essential elements of its nature.*

Psychoanalysts should not make light of inferential forms of reasoning, for it is on this form of reasoning that the value of their own conclusions largely rests. We infer contrary meanings for words that are used ostensibly in one sense, and we infer special conflicts in infancy of which we have but little evidence at hand, and cravings and passions of which it may be impossible to find more than a few traces by way of direct testimony.

Our immediate environment and the world that surrounds us in that sense, appear to our observation, indeed, as "in the making." But besides the power of observation which enables, and indeed forces us to see the imperfection in this environmental world, we possess, or are possessed by, a mental constitution which compels us, with still greater force, to the belief in a goal of positive perfection of which our nearer goals are nothing but the shadow.

It is because I believe in the necessity of such reasoning as this that I am not prepared to accept the "Lust-Unlust" principle (that is, to use philosophical terms, the "hedonistic" principle) as representing the forces by which even the child is finally animated. Men do not reach their best accomplishments, if indeed they reach any accomplishment, through the exclusive recognition, either unconscious or instinctive, of a utilitarian result, or a result which can be couched in terms of pleasure or personal satisfaction as the goal of effort. They may state the goal to themselves in these terms; but this is, then, the statement of what is really a fictitious principle, a principle in positing which the patient does but justify himself and does not define his real motive. Utilitarianism and hedonism and the pleasure-pain principle, useful though they are, are alike imperfect in that they refer to partial motives, partial forms of self-expression; whereas that which finally moves men to their best accomplishments and makes them dissatisfied with anything less than this, is the necessity rather than the desire to take complete self-expression as their final aim. The partial motives are more or less traceable as if by observation. The larger motives must be felt and reached through inferential reasoning, based on observation of ourselves through careful introspection.

Finally, the practical, therapeutic question arises, as to what measures the psychoanalyst is justified in taking to bring about the best sort of outcome in a given case?

It is widely felt that the psychoanalyst would weaken his own hold on the strong typically analytic principles through which painful conflicts are to be removed if he should form the habit of dealing with ethical issues, and talking of "duties," instead of stimulating his patients to the discovery of resistances and repressions, even of repression the origin of which is not to be found within the conscious life. Yet—parallel, as one might say, with this clear-cut standard of professional psychoanalytic obligation, the force of which I recognize—it has to be admitted that there are certain fairly definite limitations to the usefulness of psychoanalysis. As one of these limitations, well-pronounced symptoms of egoism, taking the form of narcissism, are to be reckoned. These symptoms are not easily analyzed away. But if one asks oneself, or asks one's patients, what conditions might, if they had been present from the outset, have prevented this narcissistic outcome (Jehovah type, etc.), the influence that suggests itself—looming up in large shape—is just this broad sense of ethical obligation to which repeated reference has here been made. If these patients could have had it brought home to them in childhood that they belonged, not to themselves conceived of narrowly (that is, as separate individuals) but only to themselves conceived of broadly as representatives of a series of communities taken in the largest sense, the outcome that happened might perhaps have been averted.

And what might have happened may still happen. What is to be done? Each physician must decide this for himself. He should be able both to do his best as a psychoanalyst and at the same time help the patient to free himself from that sort of repression in consequence of which he is unable to see his own best possibilities. But he cannot do this unless he has trained himself to see and feel in himself the outlines of this vision any more than he could help the patient to rid himself of an infantile complex if he did not appreciate what this complex means. We must trust ourselves, as physicians, with deadly weapons, and with deadly responsibilities, and we ought to be well harried by our consciences if we should do injustice, in using them, either to our scientific or our philosophic training.

This paper was originally read before the American Psychopathological Association on May 5, 1915. In the same year it was published in the *International Journal of Psycho-Analysis*, and in the June issue of the *Journal of Abnormal Psychology*. It also appeared in J. J. Putnam's *Addresses on Psycho-Analysis* (London and New York: International Psychoanalytic Press, 1921), and in a later edition of the same book published by the Hogarth Press and the Institute of Psycho-Analysis in 1951.

James J. Putnam was one of the first American psychiatrists to come out in favor of Freud's teachings. He met Freud during the latter's visit to this country in 1909, and exchanged numerous letters with him on the state of psychoanalysis.

Shall we have patients write down their dreams?

Karl Abraham

*A classical example of the "Kleine Mitteilung" (brief clin-
ical communication), adding new determinants to a much
over-determined, typical piece of "acting-out."*

In a short paper on "The Employment of Dream Interpretation in Psychoanalysis" (1912), Sigmund Freud briefly
considered the question of whether or not it was of advantage to let patients put down their dreams in writing,
immediately after awakening. He came to the conclusion
that such a procedure was superfluous. "Even if the substance of a dream is in this way laboriously rescued from
oblivion, it is easy enough to convince oneself that nothing
has thereby been achieved for the patient. The associations
will not come to the text, and the result is the same as if
the dream had not been preserved."

My own experience causes me fully to share this view.
The question, however, seems to me to be of considerable
interest to the psychoanalyst who in his everyday practice
makes use of the interpretation of dreams. Therefore, I
should like to bring forward certain experiences met with
in my own practice. These occurred in connection with
precisely those patients whom I had already told that it
was useless to write down their dreams.

Observation 1. A patient had a very elaborate and eventful dream associated with strong affects. Upon awakening he drowsily reached for his writing material which he had put at his bedside in spite of the analyst's instructions to the contrary. The next morning, he brought me two quarto pages full of notes. But what he had written proved to be nearly illegible. The striving to rescue the dream from oblivion obviously was countered in this case by the opposite striving (repression). The result was a compromise in that the dream actually was written down, but in illegible writing, preventing it from giving any information.

Observation 2. A patient whom in answer to his question I had warned against writing down his dreams, produced a whole series of dreams in one of the succeeding nights. Awakening in the midst of the night, he tried ingeniously to rescue from repression the dreams he considered very important. Owning a dictaphone he spoke into the machine a description of his dreams, significantly disregarding the fact that it had recently not been working properly. The record was not clear therefore. The patient had to supplement a good deal from memory. The analysis of the dream was accomplished without very much resistance. This leads me to suppose that the dream would have been preserved just as well without being recorded.

But, failing to learn from this experience, the patient tried again. The dictaphone was repaired, and gave on the morning after the dream night a rather understandable production. But, as the patient himself acknowledged, the content was so confused that he had to organize it. He succeeded in doing so, but not without difficulty. The following nights produced an abundant dream material covering the same complexes. As this could be sufficiently reproduced without any mechanical help, this case too proved the uselessness of an immediate recording of dreams.

Observation 3 proves most strikingly how useless it is to oppose by such means a powerful tendency to repression.

The patient complained for several weeks of being unable to remember a certain dream. She related that the same dream had recently recurred every night. Awakening in fright, it was her intention to tell me the dream the next morning, but each time she forgot its content. One day she told me she would keep writing material ready that night in order to be able to take notes on the dream immediately upon awakening. I advised her against this, observing that a striving which created dreams night after night would find its way into consciousness without such help; for the time being, the resistance opposing this was still too strong. She saw the point and abandoned her intention. But when she went to bed the wish to recall that night's dream returned. The patient prepared pencil and paper. She actually awoke in a state of fright from her usual dream, turned on the light, and wrote down some notes. She fell asleep again, her mind at ease in the feeling that she could no longer lose the dream. Next morning she overslept and came late to the analytic hour (resistance). She handed me a sheet of paper, saying that in her hurry she had not re-examined it that morning.

It was somewhat difficult to decipher the few words she had scribbled down, owing to the indistinct writing (see *Observation 1*). The words were these: "Write down the dream against agreement." Her resistance had won out. The patient had written down, not the dream, but only her intent of doing so. Then, satisfied with herself, she had fallen asleep.

About a week after this futile attempt she was able to relate the following dream which had occurred several times since. Its content had its source in a strong transference. The patient dreamed that I was approaching her, and each time her dream ended with her awakening in fright. The reason for keeping the dream secret ceased to exist after other symptoms of transference had made a detailed analysis of the above-mentioned incident necessary.

I should like to indicate briefly the motives which lead patients to attribute such importance to an immediate writing down of their dreams. Frequently it is a matter of transference. A patient who brings notes of a dream to the analytic hour wants (unconsciously) to prove to the analyst by means of these notes that the dream has particular reference to the latter. Sometimes a dream handed to the analyst in writing has the character of a gift presented to him, as though the patient wanted to say: "I am offering you the most precious thing I have." Obviously neurotic vanity is here involved. Many patients with pronounced narcissism are positively in love with the beauty of their dreams. They rescue them from oblivion because they consider them precious.

Just as the autoerotic neurotic likes to retain products of his body, just as he is anxious not to lose more than absolutely necessary of his bodily substance, so in the same way he is on guard that none of his intellectual products should be lost.

This paper was originally published in the *Internationale Zeitschrift für Psychoanalyse*, Vol. I, 1913. In 1914, it appeared, in a translation by Hilda Abraham, in the *International Journal of Psycho-Analysis*. It was later included in Karl Abraham's book, *Klinische Beitrage zür Psychoanalyse* (Leipzig, Vienna, Zurich: Internationaler psychoanalytischer Verlag, 1921); and in *The Psychoanalytic Reader* (New York: International Universities Press, 1948), translated by Robert Fliess.

Karl Abraham was one of the early presidents of the International Psycho-Analytic Association, and played an important role in its formative years. He was one of Freud's most esteemed pupils.

Sexuality and its role in the neuroses

A. A. Brill

In Plato's symposium we find a myth describing the ancient's attempt to explain the sexual manifestations of mankind. Man was formally a different creature, he was physically a double being, both sexes coexisting. These creatures, having become overbearing, were cut asunder by Jupiter into two halves. The skin was then pulled together and sewed up, and their heads were turned around, thus making two different sexes. Since then these two sexes have been striving to reunite. This ancient, theoretical bisexuality or hermaphroditism of man was later corroborated by science, notably through the works of Lydston and Kiernan of this country. Bisexuality exists both physically and mentally. We know that physically everything fundamental existing in the male has its analogy in the female; that it is simply a question of later development when one develops in one way, the other in the other way. This divergence had its origin at definite points in the phyletic and biontic evolution of man.

Krafft-Ebing was the first to describe sexual abnormalities from a phenomenological approach. No one ever succeeded in giving an explanation for the so-called sexual anomalies; they were looked upon as monstrosities or as peculiarities by both laymen and sexologists. Professor Freud was the first to treat psychosexuality as an integrated science. He was the first investigator to show that the roots of all sexual anomalies actually exist normally in every human being, but that due to early accidental factors, deviations or deflections from the normal path may result and do cause diversions, inversions, or deviations in reference to the sexual aim or the sexual object.[1]

According to Professor Freud, who bases his conclusions on his studies of the neurotic, the normal, and the child, there are three definite stages in the psychosexual development of man. The first stage, the autoerotic or self-gratifying age, starts with birth and continues to the age of four or five. In this stage the child shows itself as a self-satisfied individual whose outlets depend altogether on his mother; she supplies all his needs, and he seemingly craves nothing from the outer world. We call this relation of the child to the mother anaclitic, or leaning on. The child does not consider his mother as something foreign to him; he feels at one with her and considers himself, as it were, a part of her. Aside from this dependent relation, he is entirely self-sufficient, self-gratifying. We can observe him in his crib, babbling, gurgling, twisting, and rubbing his limbs, sucking his thumb, moving and swaying about in a perfectly contented manner, entirely unaware of the outside world. His mother alone supplies his hunger and his comfort cravings. This age is the most important in the child's life, for beginning with a primitive mental apparatus, all of the child's cultural foundations are laid during these first years of life.

---

[1] According to Professor Freud, the *sexual object* is the person from whom the sexual attraction emanates, while the action toward which the impulse strives he designates as the *sexual aim*.

If the first four or five years develop normally, the child will be normal. I am referring, of course, to the psychosexual development of the normal or average child.

Professor Freud's great achievement in sexology lies in the fact that he traces the sexual development to the beginning of life; the child begins with a sex life. It is true that sex in the child differs from that of the adult, but the latter is only an outgrowth of the isolated partial impulses and components which can be readily seen in the child soon after his birth. Moreover, when the average scientist or sexologist thinks of sex, he always has in mind the physical elements of sex. In this respect he differs little from the average layman to whom the word "sex" immediately conjures up something repelling, crude, and licentious, something wrong, something that must be hidden.

Our view is quite different. After a very long and deep study, Professor Freud found that the child shows a number of components and partial impulses which later enter into the formation of the normal sex instinct, for in order to attain sexual intercourse, or the *end aim* of mating, many preliminary feelings must be gratified first. The individual looks at the object and, if attracted, he says to himself, "This is a pretty girl." Following the stimulation or gratification of the sense of sight, his sense of touch comes into play. As soon as possible he desires to hold her hand; he wants to gratify his tactile sensations. If he comes in near contact with her, he may not like the odor which she emanates. Odor plays just as great a part in sexual attraction as vision and tactile sensations. As soon as she opens her mouth and begins to talk, he is also impressed by her voice. We often hear such expressions as, "Her voice is charming! How wonderful her diction!" A stimulus of one sense may sometimes suffice to start a love affair.

I can mention the case of a man who fell in love with a woman solely on account of her voice. It was in the old days, when one did not have to pay a nickel to ask the telephone operator for the time, when one could talk *ad libitum* to the telephone girl. This man accidentally discovered the operator's charming voice, and he then continually called her just to hear her talk. In time he met her and finally married her. I know that it was mainly her voice which attracted him; he confessed to me that when he first met her he was disappointed in her looks. But the voice still enchanted him. I can also tell of a physician who married a singer only because of her wonderful contralto voice. He was erotically fascinated by the voice until she died of influenza after fourteen years of a happy married existence. This doctor called on me a few years ago to discuss with me his peculiar behavior. He told me that although his wife had been in her grave for years, she indirectly still afforded him a good outlet, through a number of phonograph records of her voice. He, himself, considered this abnormal, and it is abnormal to a large extent. He ranks among those individuals who can get an outlet by looking, touching, or exhibiting—people who are known as perverts and are designated in the literature as *toucheurs, voyeurs*, etc.

To be sure, a certain amount of looking, touching, hearing, smelling, or showing off, is quite normal—nay, indispensable to man's normal sexuality, and depending on the race and the individual evolution, some senses play a greater part in mating. Thus, it would seem that nowadays the nose plays hardly any part in human mating. Closer observation, however, shows that the sense of smell is still active in the sexual life of modern man. This has been repeatedly demonstrated by very careful observers. In 1890 Fliess discovered the *Sexualstellen*—sexual spots in the nose, which he showed to have a direct connection with sexual functioning. In painful menstruation, Fliess would cocainize those spots in the nose and the pain would cease. There is an extensive literature on the subject, a large part of which was contributed by American investigators. In brief, whether we realize it or not, all the senses play a part in the sex instinct.

What is still more important is the fact mentioned above that long before the child reaches what is popularly designated as puberty, long before the function of the genitals is developed, he is a sexual being and manifests a flourishing sexuality. To be sure, the manifestations differ, for unlike the adult, the child's sexuality is independent of the genital system; the child obtains sexual outlets from various parts of the body, which Freud calls erogenous zones. The latter are not necessarily confined to the genital regions; they are parts of the body which, when stimulated, furnish sexual pleasure, and the sexual elements which emanate from them are the so-called partial impulses. The infantile sexual aim thus consists in gratification, resulting from the excitation of either the genitals, mouth, anus, or of the eyes, as in the case of looking and exhibition manias, and last but not least, of any part of the skin. As a matter of fact, experience shows that as a result of accidental factors any of the individual senses may develop into an erogenous zone.

As was mentioned above, the first period of childhood is preponderatingly autoerotic, so that the germs of sexual activity which the child brings along into the world are all of that nature. The simplest form of autoerotism manifested by the child is thumb sucking, which the child learns to enjoy while taking nourishment. In some form or other this is never given up. The adult who bites his nails, chews gum, or smokes, indulges in an autoerotic outlet, the prototype of which is thumb sucking. There are a number of other manifestations which are quite active in the same period which are unmistakably of a sexual nature. Thus, we have the component of aggression—which is destined to play a great part in both the instincts of hunger and love—the impulse of showing off or exhibitionism, the impulses for looking, touching, hearing, and smelling. Practicing mental medicine as I do, I repeatedly come across cases of sex anomalies connected with all the partial impulses. I could mention many cases treated by me because they suffered from sexual aberrations referable to all these senses. But these partial impulses or components of sex must be considered as normal in childhood. The child knows no shame or disgust, consequently he can look, touch, listen, taste, and smell everything. He wishes to see everything; he likes to show himself naked, and above all he feels no sense of sympathy, morality, or disgust. In fine, he acts and feels like any other animal.

It is because of this behavior that Professor Freud designated the child's sexual life as polymorphous perverse or perverse in all directions. But we must remember that the polymorphous perversity exists only when we consider the child's activities in the light of adult behavior, that is, if an adult behaves like the child, he is sexually abnormal. The child, however, cannot be called abnormal or immoral—at worst it is unmoral. For such behavior is as natural to the child as it is to all animals. On the other hand, an adult who is in need of such an outlet and cannot resort to the normal outlet, is sexually abnormal or perverse. A perversion is a sexual act which deviates from the normal sexual aim and can attain its outlet only through the path of a partial impulse. For although some aggression, hearing, touching, looking, tasting, smelling, and exhibiting form a necessary concomitant of normal sex, the bulk of these manifestations do not develop to the same extent as in animals and primitives. In the normal child these infantile activities are particularly repressed so that by the time they merge into the second phase of development, or the latency period, they are controlled by the so-called cultural barriers or reaction formations which have been formed by the moral and ethical restrictions of society. Sympathy, shame, modesty, disgust, and morality are the cultural dams which not only keep down the primitive partial impulses, but also enable the individual to sublimate these energies for aims other than sexual. In other words, one part is repressed, another part furnishes energy for social feelings, while the rest retains its original force, but is subjugated to the primacy of the genitals.

I cannot here enter into the evolution of the different impulses; all that I wish to emphasize is that when everything proceeds normally, the individual, so to speak, finds the sexual objects at the age of puberty. To be sure, the civilized boy or girl does not frankly manifest this need, but this is altogether due to our modern way of ignoring and suppressing the sexual functions. Behind the surface the sexual emotions are in full blast, a fact which is readily seen by any observer. However, if through some accidental factors the evolution of the sex instinct does not follow the allotted paths, a weakness or fixation may result, which may lay the foundation for a future neurosis. Or, what is worse, some of the intermediary relations to the sexual object such as touching or looking, which are preliminary pleasures leading to the sexual aim, may in themselves become the end aim, in which case we deal with a perversion. I have seen many cases of men and women in whom the primacy of the genitals has not been established, who, therefore, utilize some other part of the body for the sexual aim, or who obtain a full outlet from touching, exhibitionism, looking. The daily press not seldom reports cases of peepers (*voyeurs*), touchers (*toucheurs*), pinchers (*sadists*), or necrophilia (*craving for dead objects*), and I could report a number of cases whose fixed outlets could only be attained through kissing, to whom genital approximation was not only not desirable, but was even abhorrent.

The autoerotic phase is followed by a latency period, which is from the age of three to five or six, and which is followed in turn by the age of puberty. At this age the genitals have matured and begin to function, and the individual soon realizes that he wants a sex object from whom he eventually craves genital outlet. To be considered normal, the individual must feel a strong need for a heterosexual object with whom the sexual aim is to be attained in sexual congress. That is the biontic and immutable law which we accept as natural and desirable. Every animal is just a link, I might say a weak link, in the chain of procreation. For in nature the individual amounts to very little; the species must, however, continue at all hazards. Our effort, therefore, must be directed to assisting the child in his normal sexual development, to guiding him in his adjustment to the restraints properly imposed on all civilized beings by civilization. For any deviation from the object and aim is contrary to the scheme of nature and is bound to produce difficulties in the individual and in society. Sexual anomalies do not exist in a natural state, but observation shows that even animals may become abnormal when deprived of their love objects. In its effort to control and regulate the sex instinct society is forced to defer the legitimate mating of its members for many years, usually for at least ten years. This unnatural thwarting produces all sorts of abnormal situations, particularly in those who possess a sensitive constitution. Thus, masturbation is practically a universal practice among civilized youths, and although it is in itself harmless, it forms the *bête noire* of young people. The inadequacy of this outlet gives rise to profound mental conflicts, which form the basis of neuroses in those predisposed to them. Besides masturbation, we have prostitution, with its evil concomitants. Indeed, even a superficial study of the individual readily shows the enormous vicissitudes that he has to overcome in curbing his natural cravings to the restrictions of society. Not all can do so—some develop normally, while others develop neuroses.

Briefly, we can state that the child's sexual outlet is objectless or autoerotic, while that of the adult craves an object—his own person can no longer gratify him. We thus distinguish an ego libido[2] and an object libido. In the child we deal altogether with ego libido, but as the child grows older, the ego, which forms the great reservoir of all libido, can, and normally does, change into object libido.

The height of ego libido is attained at about the age of four or five, at the end of the autoerotic phase, when all the partial impulses and components of sex are being collected, as it were, into one bundle on the path to object finding. This short period of ego libido Freud calls the narcissistic period, because in striving for an object, the individual finds himself as the first object, that is, he becomes aware of his own person as an object of interest and love. He admires his own body, and instead of continuing to speak of himself in the third person as so many little boys

---

[2] By the term *libido* Freud designates a quantitative and changeable energy of the sexual instinct which is directed to an object. It comprises not only sexual love, but self-love, love for parents and children, friendship and devotion to concrete and abstract ideas.

are wont to do, he now begins to realize the meaning of the "ego"; and he forthwith uses the expression "I," instead of "John wants this." It is also in this period that the boy becomes interestingly aware of the importance of his genitals, and unless informed to the contrary, is firmly convinced that all individuals have the same kind of genitals. This infantile theory of sex plays a great part in male homosexuality, where the primacy of the penis is never relinquished. Freud called this period narcissistic, after a Greek youth, Narcissus, who according to the myth fell in love with his own image. The narcissistic period represents the most egotistic state of the person's existence. Normally, it is only gradually given up; the school period with its active competition, which begins about this time of life, undoubtedly helps to divert the individual from his own egotism and forces him to recognize his neighbors' rights.

In the latency period the child comes into actual contact with the outer world, and his narcissism is gradually, so to speak, knocked out of him. A certain amount of it always remains and is compatible with normal health. Self-preservation demands that the individual consider himself first; as the old Talmudic rabbis used to say, "If I am not for me, who will be for me?" The ego libido dominates childhood, but with the advance of age it is more or less controlled and displaced to other objects. This is particularly noticeable in friendship and during the state of being in love. When a man is in love in the popular sense, he throws almost all his libido on the love object. In a few days, a normal but love-stricken young man spent his whole month's salary on his best girl, and do you think he regretted it? Not at all. He was very happy over it. During the acute stage of being in love, the ego libido is at its lowest ebb. The man is then a mere worm in the dust, and the love object is on her highest level. That is why the acute stage of being in love has always been considered as abnormal; *amantes, amentes* (lovers, lunatics), and *"Amare et sapere vix deis conceditur"* (to love and to be wise is not even conceded to the gods) are old classics, the truth of which has been observed until the present day.

Libido can also be withdrawn from the outside object and turned back to the ego when for some reason the object is lost or given up. It is also a fact that object libido diminishes with age. The older a person, the less likely he is to sacrifice himself on the altar of love. The only altruism that really exists, according to Professor Freud, is the love of the mother for her little boy. Nevertheless, under normal states of development the latency period shows a gradual diminution or absorption of narcissistic or ego libido, and although the sexual manifestations seem to be dormant, one observes many signs of object finding. The young boys show an apparent dislike for the girls; they openly disparage them, while privately they begin to adore them. The young girls become more timid, more sensitive to the approach of men, and gradually begin to display all the phases of the eternal feminine.

Let us now go back again to the autoerotic stage and follow the evolution of a single component, let us say, that of aggression. A certain amount of aggression is necessary in the struggle for hunger and love. Any animal that is not aggressive will not endure very long in the struggle for existence, and everyone knows that a "faint heart never won fair lady." All male animals show an active aggressive make-up from early childhood. When a newborn boy is exhibited to relatives and friends, one often hears such expressions as "He looks like a real boy!" There is no doubt that the male animal is more aggressive than the female who is passively attractive. In fact, activity and passivity are the only distinguishing attributes in the differentiation of the two sexes. Aggression becomes more pronounced with age; at about two the little boy shows an active and destructive aggression, which we designate as the anal-sadistic organization. For if we watch a little boy at the age of about two, or even earlier, we will note that he is inexorable in his aggressive demands. He has no regard for anybody or anything; he wants everything, regardless of logic, and when thwarted, he screams, shouts, and bites. Left to himself, he would grow up as a little savage, or like a wild animal. But society, which impresses upon the child during the first four years of its life the results of many thousands of years of civilization, takes it upon itself to curb the aggressive little savage and mold him into its own pattern. When he screams, he is told to shut up, and if he persists in misbehaving, he is often spanked.

I have known of children who have been spanked by irate parents when they were only a few weeks old. But even if corporal punishment is not administered, as is now often the case, the force of the "big people" is strongly impressed upon the child. His aggression must be controlled, and, given a normal child, the outer world invariably wins. For sooner or later a reaction formation of a dam of sympathy becomes erected which henceforth holds down the aggression. The word, sympathy, comes from *syn* and *pathos*, which means to feel with or suffer with. Through continuous training the little boy is made to feel with his fellow beings; he is forced to identify himself with his neighbor's suffering. I recall a little boy who took great pleasure in throwing out of his crib a toy dog and then screaming continuously until it was returned to him. This toy dog could be made to bark through hand pressure, of which the little fellow was as yet incapable, but when he threw it out of his crib the impact of the fall made it bark. When he suddenly discovered this, he repeated the process over and over again to the annoyance of his parents, who were forced to pick it up for him. When he grew older and began to walk, he would do the same thing to his mother's pet Pomeranian. His greatest pleasure was to throw the dog off his chair so as to make it yelp, and despite repeated admonitions, he repeated it whenever possible. This mischievous action gave him great pleasure because it made him conscious of his power. His mother loved her pet. Consequently, she often chided him for maltreating it. She even strove to instill in her little boy a love for dogs; she would often say, "Pet the doggie, nice little doggie," all of which was of no avail. One day when he again abused the dog the mother lost her patience and knocked him down, saying "What you do to the dog, I will do to you." The little fellow cried his heart out, but the mother tells me that he never abused her pet again; in fact, he now loves the dog, who is his constant companion. By her act of violence the mother actually forced the child to "feel with" or to empathize himself into the dog, and thus erected a dam against his primitive cruelty. Sympathy is the reaction formation that holds down the innate cruelty. Every civilized being shows this reaction to his primitive aggression. We do not like to see people suffer; we do not even like to maltreat animals, because we feel with them. We unconsciously identify ourselves with them.

If the aggression has not been properly repressed, a weak spot or a fixation may result through some accidental experiences. There may have been a lack of curbing, too much punishment by parents, or long and persistent suffering through diseases of early childhood. The resulting reaction formation in all such cases must be correspondingly strong. Thus, I can mention a number of people who were active workers against cruelty to animals—one a well-known anti-vivisectionist—who were in childhood extremely cruel to animals, or were treated cruelly by parents. One of these patients was so extreme in his feelings that he became a vegetarian. He is now in a quandary because someone told him that plants, too, live and feel. He simply cannot accept the natural law that everything living must live on something living.

The anal-sadistic stage is so designated because at the age when the child evinces marked aggressive tendencies, he also expresses himself forcibly through his anal functions. For the first ego organizations of the child are expressed by the mouth and the anus. The mouth, or oral organization, which can be observed at a very early age, already expresses the child's characteristic ego. Many children bite their mothers' nipples; this is particularly true of boys. I have a large collection of notes brought by mothers which tell of their experiences with breast biting. Girls also bite, but boys bite more than girls for both defense and attack. Children also express their pleasure and spite through their mode of taking nourishment. They refuse to take nourishment when they are irritable and displeased with the parent, and when forced to take food will frequently refuse to swallow it. I have seen children who have kept food in their mouths for twenty-four hours and longer just for spite. They not only deliberately refuse to swallow food, but often vomit it up after they have been compelled to eat. This oral resistance displayed in early life is frequently repeated later in adult life. Loss of appetite, nausea, vomiting, and other gastrointestinal disturbances form the most frequent symptoms in the psychoneuroses.

The next ego manifestations, which are even more important for normal development, are those connected with the anus and its activities. Civilization demands that we lead a sanitary existence, that the excrements should be properly disposed of, and after thousands of years we have developed disgust, which is one of the most potent reaction formations against the interest and pleasure in the excrements. If an individual possesses no disgust, he is surely not normal, and if he is incapable of developing it, he is mentally on a low level. For it is the feeling of disgust that keeps us from indulging in the polymorphous perversities of childhood.[3] To the child, feces constitute a valuable possession in which he is interested until he develops the reaction formation. Nevertheless, even in adults disgust for feces and their odor is more apparent than real. One is surprised to find that people like to linger in the toilet much longer than necessary. They frequently sit there and read, and I have known some who referred to their luxuriously furnished closets as "the library." It would seem then that people are disgusted only by the excrementitious odors of others, but not by their own.

However, sanitation demands early training for the control of anal and urethral functions, and parents, therefore, begin to regulate them at the beginning of childhood. Pediatricians take due note of this need, and some have devised special ways of training. I recall that in my student days I heard Dr. Holt recommend that mothers insert a glass rod and stimulate the anus at regular intervals in order to establish a certain regularity in the movement of the bowels. Within the last five years I have had two patients who were started as neurotics in this very way. In addition to other

---

[3] There are also ethnic reasons why we control the disposal of the excrements, reasons into which we cannot delve here.

symptoms, they were both marked anal erotics. To be sure, Dr. Holt was entirely unaware of the permanence of early infantile impressions and their harm in predisposed persons; what he wished to bring about was the control of what modern homes consider disagreeable habits. Parents exert more emotional feeling in the training of the child's bowel control than in any other function. The little boy has to empty his bowels before he is put to bed; otherwise, the household routine would be disturbed—but no child wants to be put to bed. Hence, the child frequently refuses compliance. But civilization is based on strict regulations and cooperation—we have to eat at a certain time, go to bed at a certain time, and attend to our natural wants at a specific time. One forever hears in the nursery such expressions as, "Do your duty," or "Do number two," or some other cryptic expression. The home routine for the night must be put into operation, the child must be put to sleep. The mother or nurse wishes to go out, but before doing so must make sure that the child will not meet with an accident during sleep. As the grownups are so eager to obtain from the child his excrement, the child soon becomes alive to its importance. He thinks that it must be something very valuable; otherwise, his mother or nurse would not be so anxious for it. Feces then becomes a symbol of power, for through the anal function the child can express spite and resistance. Moreover, the child actually derives pleasure from defecation, especially when he is slightly constipated, so that he likes to linger at the act. If the child is angry or does not wish to be put to bed, he refuses to empty his bowels.

Right from the beginning every child endeavors to express himself as a free and independent being, and the oral and anal activities are the first two ego organizations which serve this purpose. Through them he shows his resistances and contempt for the rules and regulations which are foreign to his primitive nature. But, as said above, in the normal child the reaction formations of sympathy, disgust, and morality soon develop, and these cultural dams tame the primitive aggression and subject the natural functions to proper control. The child then shows pity, modesty, shame, and a sense of cleanliness—attributes which are absolutely necessary for civilized life. One of the surest diagnostic signs of mental deficiency is a general incapacity to develop these dams. But, even in the average child, fixations or weak spots, resulting from accidents, remain places of least resistance to which libido may later regress. In such cases the main stream of libido, which is normally directed to object finding, is weakened, and we may have a perversion such as sadism, or the negative of the perversion, a neurosis. In the latter case, instead of exercising pathological aggression on animals or human beings, the constitutionally predisposed person develops symptoms in the form of phobias, doubts, and obsessions. Instead of consciously desiring to hurt or torture, as in the case of sadism, the obsessive neurotic forever fears that he may be the cause, directly or indirectly, of injury or death. A pin from his shirt might be swallowed by a child with fatal results; he might pick up germs from a door knob and infect others with tuberculosis or syphilis, etc., etc. There is no end to the tortures and misfortunes that he might cause to others. Or by the same reasoning, all these misfortunes may be directed to his own person. In that case the patient takes himself as the object of aggression. The neurosis, according to Professor Freud, is thus the negative of the perversion.

To sum up, we can say that all sexual manifestations, be they normal or abnormal, have their origin in the sexual activities of childhood. Normally these activities gradually undergo a definite development and the individual can then function in a normal sexual manner. Any sensitive child subjected for a time to certain impressions may either be impeded or prevented from reaching the normal goal, and may then be sexually below par or sexually abnormal. I wish to emphasize the fact that a poor environment has nothing to do with the situation. On the contrary, my records show that perversions and inversions are more likely to happen in very fine home environments. Only sons are in a more favorable environment for homosexuality than those who have siblings. Pathological peeping and exhibitionism never develop in homes where there is sexual frankness. All of my cases belonged to homes where the utmost care was exercised to keep the child from seeing the sexual elements exposed. Nor are sexually abnormal people mentally or emotionally degenerate as so many physicians and laymen believe. As a rule, my cases were above the average in mental equipment. But it must not be forgotten that the defectives are also invariably abnormal in their sex life. In other words, sex is a natural instinct which must be definitely developed to meet the unnatural environment of civilization. Freud deserves the greatest credit for showing us the whole development of this instinct, so that we can now understand the relation between the normal, the pervert, and the neurotic.

BIBLIOGRAPHY

Brill, A. A. "The Sense of Smell in the Neuroses and Psychoses," *The Psychoanalytic Quarterly*, I (April, 1932), i.
———. "Necrophilia," *J. of Criminal Psychol.* Vols. II and III.
Freud, Sigmund. *Three Contributions to the Theory of Sex.* Tr. by A. A. Brill. New York: E. P. Dutton, 1963.

This article first appeared in the *International Journal of Psycho-Analysis* in 1932. It was subsequently included in *Psychoanalysis Today*, edited by Sandor Lorand (New York: Covici-Friede, 1933), and in a later edition of the same book, also edited by Sandor Lorand (International Universities Press, 1944).

A. A. Brill is one of the pioneers of American psychoanalysis. He translated a number of Freud's works, among which are *Interpretation of Dreams* and *Three Contributions to the Theory of Sex*. He was one of the founders of the American Psychoanalytic Association.

The wish to be a man

Hanns Sachs

The patient whose case I am presenting was a very intelligent young girl aged about twenty, belonging to a refined and religious family. She came for analysis not on account of any strongly marked neurotic symptoms, but because she was burdened by uncertainty and anxiety, and was unable to concentrate her thoughts or form plans for the future, although her difficulties were not sufficiently great completely to prevent her carrying out her duties. It was only later on, after the analysis had progressed considerably, that she recalled a marked neurotic symptom which had appeared after puberty (at about the age of fourteen), and had become repressed again, namely, the obsessional idea (which had caused her much suffering), that when she walked out of doors all the passers-by could see her genital organs. At the very beginning, when I asked her to tell freely all her thoughts, she declared, after some hesitation and with all the signs of an inward struggle, that she felt unable to comply with the fundamental principle of psychoanalysis (*i.e.* to utter everything which came into her mind) until she had made a full confession of something that had oppressed her ever since her youth. When she was aged twelve and a half she had spent some months in the house of an aunt, and a boy cousin, about a year older than herself, had been her playmate. In those games which had a sexual background, the kind common among children of this age, these two had gone rather far in overt action. Beginning with merely viewing and touching each other's genitals, they had arrived finally very near to the act of sexual intercourse. I was obliged to piece together all this from the hints she dropped, for though my patient was too intelligent to be a prude in the ordinary sense, nevertheless she could not bring herself to relate these incidents clearly and coherently. I surmised, and my guess was confirmed by the patient herself, that she was oppressed by the fear of having lost her virginity at this time. After this episode she had experienced great depression, feeling herself morally depraved and unworthy to mix with her sisters and comrades. She had never confided in anyone, and her mother was the only person who knew anything about the matter. When I asked how her mother, who had not been present at the time, came to know about it, she replied in an astonished way that she really did not know—it had never occurred to her before to consider that question. In addition, she told me that since her early childhood she had not been on very confidential terms with her parents who were too pious and narrow-minded for her. As a result of these wrongdoings in childhood she developed an abhorrence of sexuality in actual life and in art, and an intense dislike to being touched, still more to being kissed, by a man. At her sister's wedding she hid herself immediately after the ceremony to avoid kissing her new brother-in-law. She could never listen when her comrades spoke of sexual matters, and she declared that she was eighteen when she learned for the first time, at college, of the difference between the male and female genitals, of the facts of procreation, and of childbirth. At this stage I interrupted her with the remark that her experiences with her cousin should have sufficed to open her eyes as to the difference between the two sexes. She still, nevertheless, firmly maintained that she had remained ignorant of these facts until her eighteenth year, although she could not herself reconcile this with her earlier experiences.

I wish to point out here that this is a typical instance of a repression which did not completely succeed. The traumatic occurrence itself remained in consciousness, but all connecting associations with the rest of the conscious mind were completely eradicated, and the tendency to throw off this memory had thereby hindered her from profiting by it to obtain knowledge on sexual matters. Further we shall see shortly that her memory of this significant occurrence was far from being complete, but as regards some important points had failed her owing to the repressing tendency.

During the first interview, which lasted two hours, I was struck by a peculiarity of my patient—one which made rather large demands upon my self-control. This was her quite extraordinary restlessness: sometimes she would throw herself to the right side, then to the left; or, lying on her back, she would draw her feet upwards and throw them straight out again suddenly; sometimes she sat up to straighten her dress, or fidgeted along the wall with her hands, or played with her handkerchief, or fumbled in her hair, and so forth. I finished this sitting with some quieting explanations which made some impression upon her, but neither then, nor later, was her general condition changed, nor her unrest. During this first interview she related to me her earliest remembrance: a stranger (a man) had taken her on his knee and she had bitten his ear. In every way she had been a wild child. She would never play with dolls, and for playfellows she chose, not girls, but the wildest and most unruly boys, with whom she tried to compete. After this narration she gave vent to complaints—often repeated in subsequent sittings—concerning her feeling of inferiority as a woman. She thought that the best and cleverest of the young men with whom she was acquainted would refuse to accept a girl as a real comrade, or to let her share in their serious masculine interests. A superficial observer would have deduced that this inferiority feeling was the core of her depressed condition.

The second interview brought about two important communications. Since the previous sitting, the patient had—without any orders from me, naturally—inquired of her mother how she had come to know about the episode with the cousin. The mother had given the surprising answer that my patient herself had confessed all, apparently without external reason, shortly after the occurrence, when the family moved to a new residence. A second communication made to me by my patient was that although she was accustomed to sleep long hours and deeply, she was very restless, sometimes tossing about, talking, and even getting up in her sleep without knowing it. Further, that the night after our first interview a very curious thing had occurred. When she was called in the morning, it was found that she had got up during the night in her sleep and had bolted the door. This was easily interpreted as a transference, by way of unconscious fantasies, of her youthful sexual experiences on to the person of the analyst, and the matter of the transference having thus started favorably, the work of analysis proceeded quickly.

After three months of analysis we reached a phase in which the patient always told her dreams (which she remembered very clearly) without being able to give any useful associations, so that the interpretation remained very incomplete. The theme of these dreams was always some forbidden act carried out by the dreamer: once she dreamed that she entered a house against the will of the owner, and another time that she stole flowers from someone's garden. After some time had been spent in endeavoring to interpret her dreams, there suddenly came to the surface a remembrance, repressed hitherto, which contained a most important part of the patient's sexual life. She now quite clearly remembered that about the age of fifteen or sixteen every night in bed she had a vision that Christ lay at her side and repeated with her the sexual acts she had experienced with her cousin, so that she felt a very vivid sexual excitation. Although this fantasy was so repulsive to her that she dreaded to go to sleep, she gave way to it for some time. Such a fantasy is a typical offspring of infantile masturbation, and very likely in the course of the fantasy masturbation was actually carried out unconsciously by pressing together the thighs, although of this the patient had no recollection.

After having produced this remembrance, she at once came to another theme which seemed closely associated with the former. She related that her first menstruation had taken place a short time after her return home from the visit to her aunt; she knew no details about the occurrence, only that somehow she had been very much surprised by it. She remembered also that her elder sister had told her that she had been on a visit when the first menstruation suddenly appeared, and had been so much taken by surprise that she had called for help.

The Christ fantasy was the first instance of masturbation which came back to the patient's consciousness, and now the connection between the different facts, hitherto so obscure, became quite clear. By means of the erotic scenes with her cousin her sexuality had been prematurely aroused in a high degree. After separation from her companion there was no other way open to her to satisfy her roused desires save by masturbation. When the first menstruation appeared, she saw in the sudden flow of blood a punishment for her misuse of her genital organs, and in her terror and contrition was impelled to confess to her mother her secret misdeeds with her cousin. The remembrance of her sister's great fright over her first menstruation was a so-called "cover memory" for the since repressed disturbances in her own mind over the similar experience of her own. There remained only one open question, and others, more definite, followed later on. Why was it that the terror roused by the bleeding genital had been so strong and remained unmitigated, although without doubt the mother had explained that this was quite a normal occurrence?

The material I had previously obtained allowed a conjecture on the question. I knew already that she had a vague remembrance of something that had happened in the days of her early childhood when she was about four or five years old. She knew that she had done something of a forbidden and sexual character with a boy playmate of the same age. In telling about this she discovered in her memory—without the slightest idea of its meaning, or where she had picked it up—the vulgar word for the sexual act in the language of the country where she had lived from her birth until her tenth year. I thought it justifiable to assume that at this time (of the forbidden act) she had seen her playfellow's genital organ and this had caused her envy. She had naturally asked herself why she was lacking in this important part, and had given herself the answer that it had been somehow taken away from her as a punishment for misusing it. This experience, therefore, would have been the prototype of the later sexual acts with her cousin, and the source of her anxiety. It tallied well with my conjecture that she had (as I heard later on), about the same time, tried by every means in her power to annoy her nursemaid; although ordinarily very kindhearted, she had behaved most cruelly to this person, without any conscious motive. Probably a threat used by the nurse in connection with the patient's infantile onanism had aroused this hatred. This conjecture I communicated to her with all possible caution. She remained silent for a long time, and then asked suddenly: "What is the meaning of biting one's own hand?" I answered her by another question, namely, whether in this case, "one" did not stand for "I." I added: "If you have this habit you will understand it now, without my help." In reply she gave the interpretation to be as follows: She had believed earlier that her male genital organ had been bitten off.

I will point out here that this belief, curious as it may seem, must once have been very widespread. Numerous ethnological parallels exist: a great majority among primitive peoples hold that a woman in menstruation has been bitten in the genital organs by some demon.

The earliest remembrance from her childhood is therefore a "cover memory," serving to obliterate from her memory the most painful impression, and substituting for the idea of being bitten the opposite idea of biting. This turning of passivity into activity became an important character trait. Henceforward biting was an unconscious outcome of her repressed tendencies, and in satisfying these she punished herself by hurting the hand—the instrument of her early guilt. This, too, was the reason why she was unable to kiss, even on such a formal occasion as her sister's wedding.

From all this, the envy regarding men and inferiority feeling of the patient and her desire to be a man are revealed in quite a new light. That we had discovered the truth was demonstrated by the result: from this moment her restless-less entirely disappeared. Without having formed any plan, without struggle or exertion, she was able to lie motionless and continued to do so, excepting on certain occasions of great emotional stress, during the remainder of the analysis.

This article appeared in 1920 in the *Internationale Zeitschrift für Psychoanalyse* and in the *International Journal of Psycho-Analysis*, Vol. I, 1920, in a translation by Barbara Low.

Hanns Sachs was one of Freud's earliest followers and pupils. Throughout Freud's life, Sachs remained a loyal adherent of his teachings. He founded, after the German *Imago* had ceased to appear, the American *Imago*, and was its editor until his death.

Remarks on lay analysis

Max Eitingon

The recent discussion on lay analysis has resulted in many quarters (especially amongst our English colleagues) in a very thorough and detailed consideration of most of the factors which have to be taken into account, and also, on the other hand, in a simple and descriptive elaboration of the main problem (Dr. Horney). Having followed the discussion attentively, we shall note that there are two points to be stressed when we realize that we are dealing with the therapeutic application of analysis and with a question relating to our training technique: namely, what conditions are to be imposed on candidates who aspire to train as practicing analysts? In the discussion the desirability has so far never seriously been questioned—on the contrary it has in general been more or less expressly emphasized—of such candidates having a preliminary training in medicine, which should be as good as possible. On the other hand it is admitted on all sides that a whole series of psychoneuroses, and precisely those which come within the true sphere of psychoanalysis as a therapy, can be successfully treated not only by physicians, but by trained non-medical practitioners, provided only that they are thoroughly instructed in analysis. Upon the opportunity for such training hangs not only the future of psychoanalysis as a form of treatment, but also as a science with all its possible applications, whether already initiated or still to be developed in the future. To provide these opportunities of training has, therefore, of late years been the principal task and the most pressing care of our organization, and particularly of the body created by it for this purpose, namely, the International Psycho-Analytical Training Commission. Now, if our candidates are to be well taught, we must give the fullest consideration not only to improving the training in our own science, which is so fundamentally novel and revolutionary, but also to the individual requirements of the special fields of knowledge to which we desire to teach students to apply analysis. For there we have to deal with branches of learning and orders of facts which are, so to speak, pre- and extra-analytical—are so inevitably, and for the most part must remain so.

I have said that it can hardly be doubted, from any point of view, that there are many very important psychoneuroses which can be successfully treated by trained non-medical practitioners who are thoroughly instructed in analysis. Nevertheless, all parties have made it no less clear that, even in such cases, the non-medical analyst must be assisted both before and during the analysis by a physician, and by this we mean naturally a physician versed in analysis. It will be his business to diagnose and to decide on the advisability of treating a patient by analysis and, further, to give his opinion on intercurrent somatic complications which may arise during the analysis. In other words, we can only conceive of the lay analyst in association with his medical colleague and as working in cooperation with him. Is it altogether utopian to suggest that what we have to aim at, if there is to be a more ideal state of affairs in the future, is that the practicing analyst's plan of procedure and training should be so framed as to substitute for the cooperation of non-medical analyst and physician the combination in a single person of an equally good analytical and medical training?

In making this suggestion I am constantly bearing in mind that, while thus practically desiring to anticipate a better future, we must give due value to two considerations, if the progress of psychoanalysis is not to be seriously impeded. In the first place we must never for a moment lose sight of the fact, and the reasons underlying it, that, within a very short time of the inception of what we call the psychoanalytical movement, a number of "laymen" were rendering the most valuable services in its further development on both the theoretical and the practical sides, and that they have continued to do so right up to the present day.

On the other hand, we must not for an instant forget the present unsatisfactory state of affairs in medicine, both from the purely scientific and the instructional point of view. We must continually keep alive and foster this dissatisfaction with a system by which psychological considerations are held at arm's length from, or repudiated by, medicine, if they have not previously been stifled by it.

Having regard to the particular requirements of the special task under discussion, the present inadequacy of medical training and the hope that at a time not too far distant we may look for its reformation, we are venturing in the name of the International Psycho-Analytical Training Commission to lay before the Congress the two following resolutions:

1. The Congress instructs the Training Committees of the Branch Societies to insist that candidates for training in psychoanalytic therapy shall possess or shall acquire full medical qualifications, but that no candidate shall be rejected solely on the ground of the lack of such qualifications, if he possesses special personal suitability and a previous scientific education of a corresponding standard.

2. While this is the general principle to be observed, each Branch Society shall determine independently its conditions of admission to training. In the case of candidates from a foreign country the conditions laid down by the Training Committee in his native country are to be taken into account together with those valid in the other country, and the Training Committee of the candidate's country is then to be notified that he has been accepted. Any protests are to be addressed to the International Training Commission.

This paper appeared in the *Internationale Zeitschrift für Psychoanalyse* in 1927, and was published under the title "Concluding remarks on the question of lay analysis" in the *International Journal of Psycho-Analysis*, Vol. VIII, 1927. The translator is unknown.

Max Eitingon was especially active in the formative years of the International Psycho-Analytic Association, and was considered a close associate of Freud's. He was identified with the founding and development of the psychoanalytic movement in Germany.

Telepathy and psychoanalysis

Eduard Hitschmann

I

Clairvoyant perception of a distant balloon accident

In the year 1910 a great sensation was made in the principal town of one of the Austrian provinces by two young men who had constructed a dirigible balloon. Local patriotism gave enthusiastic expression to its pride in the first Austrian balloon of the dirigible type; there was also, however, a note of skepticism in the newspapers. The balloon had no valve and therefore could not be made to descend in case of an accident; in the heat of strong sunshine it might fly to an enormous height and possibly burst. It was later brought to Vienna and one Saturday made a successful ascent, the Emperor being a spectator; the present writer then read an account of this with rising interest and looked at its photograph in an illustrated paper, at the same time, however, feeling some disappointment that so much recognition should be accorded to a type of aircraft by no means high in technical efficiency. On the following Sunday I thought more than once of going to see the second ascent, but allowed various things to prevent me. At about the time when the balloon was to go up I was sitting at table, when suddenly, looking at the clock, I called out, "It is half-past three—one of the brothers is falling out of the balloon which is being carried away!" I had a vision of this happening as I spoke.

Three hours later I heard in the street that this had actually happened, and that the balloon with one of its pilots had been carried high into the air, landing later on without further mishap not far from Vienna. I had a feeling of satisfaction and of amazement at my capacity for foreseeing future events; the only disturbing element was the fact that the balloon had collided against the hangar, so that the aviator had not fallen but had been flung out, which I had never thought of.

In view of the improbability of anyone suddenly describing in a prophetic way an event taking place an hour's journey distant and seeing it before his very eyes, we may regard this case as a fresh proof of the possibility of clairvoyance.

II

Telepathic intimation of a father's death

The poet Max Dauthendey, in his autobiographical work *Der Geist meines Vaters*, gives an account of the telepathic intimations that he received of his father's death. He writes as follows:

> For some time the son had been interested in occult phenomena, the symbolism of numbers, and so on. One day he was playing with a so-called "star card," i.e., two concentric circular cards of different sizes, on the smaller of which is a chart of the constellations and the Milky Way, whilst on the margin of the larger card are marked the three hundred and sixty-five days of the year. By placing any given

day on the meridian of the "star card" the position of the constellations on that day can be seen. He now "in imagination" placed it on the date of his father's birthday and then on that of his own, saw with amazement that the tracks of the Milky Way intersected at these two dates, and wondered to himself whether this signified the contrast between his own nature and his father's. At that moment for no external reason he suddenly experienced a very distinctive hallucination, which persisted for some time, of a smell of tobacco which he remembered from the days of his youth as characteristic of his father. At the moment he was just going to wash his hands; and feeling that the smell proceeded from them, he washed them several times over. It proved, however, to be an hallucination, for his wife declared emphatically that there was no such smell perceptible. Several hours later the poet received at his address in Paris a telegram stating that his father had died at home in Würzburg at the very hour when the hallucination of tobacco had occurred in Paris. This event, which took place in September, produced in the son a feeling of solemnity rather than grief; it followed upon a dream which he had had three months before containing an intimation of his father's death. In the month of June the younger Dauthendey had suddenly started up from his sleep (he was lying stretched out like a corpse with his hands folded on his breast) and heard a voice saying, "In September your father will die!" On that occasion too he had not felt any grief, only a sensation of shuddering awe at the impressive tidings of death. The poet made a note of this dream in his diary, and as the month of September approached he and his wife recalled the prophecy; the death foretold actually occurred on the fifth of September. Would anyone be prepared to deny that in this instance the accumulated operation of strange influences from afar points to the assumption of mystical forces at work?

III

Clairvoyance and telepathy in popular opinion

We have here two cases of clairvoyance and telepathy, one of which was observed by the writer of these pages, being himself the percipient; whilst the other is described in detail by a well-known poet in an autobiographical work. The one is a case of the perception and knowledge of a flying accident which took place many miles away, whilst the other is an experience of a son's receiving while in Paris strange intimations of the death of his father living in Würzburg. Reports of similar observations are no longer rare; in the press and in the various collected works of Flammarion, Hyslop and others, there are many instances of clairvoyance, telepathy, intimations of death and prophecies, though it is true these examples are always given in quite a brief form. Hence the majority of my readers are not at all likely to refuse to accept such cases of telesthesia as facts. It is easy enough at the present day to fall back on the banal explanation, "Well, there is such a thing as wireless telegraphy!" Might not the minds of father and son be so attuned to one another that the son could be aware of emanations from his father's mind, especially in the supreme hour of death? It is possible that a minority of my readers may be more skeptical and deny such happenings; it is not pleasant to see the facts of physics and physiology go by the board. Superstition confronts us on every side. Mediums have often enough been shown up as frauds at spiritistic séances; a poet may well be regarded as an untrustworthy witness it is his very profession to put his fantasies on record. Finally, there are cautious men of science who shake their heads when they hear of such marvels, and go back to their work of exact investigation, saying: "Of course it is possible that there are forces of which as yet we know nothing, but I shall wait till I have better evidence. Your accounts are superficial; you must make more exact inquiries; take note of time and place; above all, observe the *mental condition* of the person who has had the telepathic experience."

This method of exact examination of the details is the one we shall pursue here.

IV

Analysis of the mental condition of the percipient in the case of the balloon accident

It is obvious that such traces of telesthesia must be examined immediately; the traces they leave are only too easily obliterated by time. I subjected my clairvoyant knowledge of the flying accident to a thorough analysis then and there, and now give the result as follows:

The actual event took place half an hour *later* than the vision; and one of the pilots had been flung out, owing to the balloon's colliding with the hangar, instead of falling out, according to the hallucination. Someone with an especially mystical turn of mind might indeed go so far as to suggest that the occurrence was the consequence of this wicked thought! But against this we must remember how many more people cherished the hope that everything would go well.

Let us analyze in greater detail my state of mind on that particular day. My attitude toward the ascent of the balloon was that of great interest; at the same time, since I had stayed away owing to my own indecision, I had a certain grudge against it. When I looked at the clock at half-past three I must have suddenly realized that it was now out of the question for me to witness the ascent. A feeling of skepticism due to the imperfections of this form of aircraft confirmed me in the fantasy that the ascent would be a failure—a fantasy that had haunted me for the last day or two. At the moment when I saw the vision, which I recounted half in jest to my brother, I selected one of my various fantasies on the subject of the failure of the ascent. One of these fantasies, namely, that excessive exposure to the sun might lead to a catastrophe, I rejected in my own mind because the autumn sunshine was not very strong. The malicious wish that the sight I had missed should end in disaster may also have been conditioned by the fact that my original intention to spend Sunday in feminine society had not been fulfilled. The circumstance that my fantasy took the form of a vision may perhaps be explained by my having been reading that morning about clairvoyant experiences of this sort, and by having perhaps unconsciously hoped to meet with some such experience myself. Further, the momentary character of the vision reminds us of the form of a witticism. We have only to imagine that the actual occurrence did not follow the vision and we see that my remark about one of the pilots having fallen out, etc., would simply have been a "bad joke," a piece of gratuitous malice, which would certainly have betrayed some personal feeling. It was rather like the way in which the Viennese often grumble: "It will turn out badly right enough!" I may add that jokes do occur to me quite often and that very frequently they are of an aggressive nature. The psychologist Freud has elucidated brilliantly the relations of aggressive wit to the unconscious mental life of the person making the joke. A joke affords an opportunity for giving vent to repressed complexes. In wit the aggressive instinct which is at other times inhibited finds partial gratification. The hallucinatory form of the words "now . . . he is falling . . ." also reminds us of dreams, which (as Freud again has demonstrated in his famous work *Interpretation of Dreams*) stand in the most intimate relation to unconscious wishes and regularly transform thoughts into sensory images.

A more profound self-analysis enables me to add the following remarks. I was thirty-nine years old at the time, and a bachelor; I and a brother two years my junior were living with our mother. The three of us were on the best possible terms; but, at the same time, a certain jealousy existed between us brothers (based on former rivalry), the points at issue being, on the one hand, our affectionate care for our mother and, on the other, our right to be free from claims in the home on Sundays, especially in the afternoons, to spend the time as we chose according to the dictates of friendship or love.[1] On Sunday afternoons we both harbored conflicting desires to be free and to do our duty by keeping our mother company. Supposing I had stayed at home, it rather annoyed me if my brother were there too. An impatient feeling—"You or I"—was in the air—"One in and the other out." The analogy to the subject of the vision is very obvious.[2]

---

[1] Cf. Sándor Ferenczi, "Sunday Neuroses" in his *Final Contributions to the Problems and Methods of Psychoanalysis* (New York: Basic Books, 1955), pp. 174–177.

[2] To this interpretation I subjoin the following additional remarks, hardly suitable for the general public. It is improbable that any other occasion than that of a flying exhibition would have given rise to this pseudo-clairvoyant experience. As the psychoanalytic interpretation of dreams has shown, an air balloon, particularly in the form in which it appeared to the percipient in this

From what I have said it is now quite clear that we have here an instance of a "curse" of some kind finding expression. We have, however, to explain how anyone accustomed to scientific thinking could at that moment imagine that his ejaculation could bring about a distant event and have a disastrous influence on the ascent of the balloon. We are reminded of the magic spells of superstitious primitive peoples, to which they ascribe power to influence the outside world. Narcissism is the term applied by Freud to the savage's overestimation of himself, which leads him to attribute to himself "omnipotence of thought." He believes that his thoughts are able to kill a foe and to bring about fortune or misfortune.

In concluding these remarks on the clairvoyant premonition of the balloon accident, I will ask my readers the following question: Which seems the more probable, that I was endowed at that particular moment with the extraordinary capacity of perceiving by telepathy a quite unimportant event which took place many miles away half an hour later in time? Or that the following psychological explanation is the right one: that I was full of feelings of skepticism, hostility and self-reproach; dissatisfied with myself and irritated by the society of my family, which I found

---

instance, is a symbol for the male organ. Bound up with the male's jealousy of other males, there are intimate associations of the ideas of comparison of one's own penis with that of others, destruction of another's penis and, so to speak, of placing another under the curse of impotence. The percipient in this case can recall a dream from his bachelor days, which was occasioned by moving into another house on account of which (the new country house being smaller than their old home) he had to sleep with his brother, as they had done in childhood, instead of having a separate room. On the first night in the new home he dreamt of striking at a serpent. The gondola in which the pilots of an airship sit is, in the language of the unconscious, symbolic of the mother's womb.

dull and irksome on a Sunday afternoon; annoyed at the presence of my brother who was only too much like myself; and disappointed both at having failed to go and see the ascent of the balloon and at having my hopes in love frustrated; and that in consequence I rid myself of these oppressive and conflicting unconscious feelings by means of a spiteful and revengeful vision? In this way I succeeded in spoiling for the other two their enjoyment of their Sunday afternoon, in justifying my not having gone to see the balloon, in giving vent to my jealousy of my brother and in gaining relief from the accumulated inner tension. There were so many motives and they were so strong that they gave rise not merely to a thought but to an hallucination, which my vanity took the risk of recounting to my companions. I seem to have attributed to myself for one moment omnipotence of thought, the capacity of clairvoyance, and the power of exercising a magical influence at a distance.

v

Analysis of the mental attitude in the son who received
an intimation of his father's death

Dauthendey's works provide ample material for the psychological interpretation of his premonitions of his father's death.

The relations between the elder Dauthendey and his two sons were similar and yet different. The elder brother could not get on at all with his father, who was capable of inflicting the most cruel punishments upon his sons. From the very beginning this brother's attitude toward his father was one of masculine defiance; and there came a day when the son suddenly took his departure, saying that he could not work near his father. Subsequently he went to Holland and America, and two years later shot himself, being afflicted with delusions of persecution.

With the other son, who was eight years younger and gifted with poetic talents, things were different. His was a gentler nature and his father felt more tenderly toward him, seeing in him the image of his wife who had died young. The two often went for walks, when the father would engage in intimate talk with him. To all appearance this boy was the favorite child, but there was one point on which father and son differed profoundly: from childhood the latter was a dreamer, whilst the former manifested the utmost antagonism and intolerance toward the habit of dreaming, with which he constantly reproached his son and which he tried to drive out of him by means of cold baths and gymnastic exercises.[3] Of a softer and more submissive disposition than his brother, the younger son, in spite of

---

[3] The poet speaks of these daydreams of his in an entirely characteristic manner: "When my father insisted that I should give up dreaming I felt as if my heart were being torn out of my body ... but just as nobody could order me to sleep without dreaming, so, as I soon sorrowfully realized, though I could certainly force myself to work, dreams rose up in my brain in the daytime, when I was awake, no less unconsciously than at night when I was asleep ... and in the midst of my work, in the midst of writing my school tasks, or listening to what was being said ... I could not help my mind being suddenly far away from the classroom, my ears hearing voices speaking, my eyes looking on landscapes, my feet wandering on woodland paths, whilst I listened to the ringing of bells and in my mind lived with people out of the stories I had read; and then, suddenly back in the classroom, I found that I had lost the thread."

Cf. Freud, "The Relation of the Poet to Daydreaming," *Collected Papers*, Vol. IV, tr. by I. F. Grant Duff (New York: Basic Books, 1959); also Hitschmann, "Zum Werden des Romandichters," *Imago*, Vol. I, No. 1, and "Gottfried Keller," *Internationale psychoanalytische Bibliothek*, No. 7.

the strongest feelings of resistance against his father and in spite of plans to escape (he wanted against his father's will to be an artist, or later on a poet), remained in bondage at home and succeeded his father as head of his tedious business as a photographer. Not until he was in the twenties did he one day confront him and declare that he must leave the house, that for years he had been living a wasted life. For the past three months he had hardly spoken to his father, except to answer Yes and No. "For," as we read in his book, "the pressure his spirit exerted upon mine wearied me to death."

It is quite easy to recognize here the ambivalence of the son's attitude: on the one hand, in his need for love the motherless boy depended on his father, whilst on the other he felt himself oppressed by him. Full of the longing for freedom and of his plans for poetic activity, at last he painfully extricated himself from the home and went out into the world. Years afterward he came back as a distinguished poet to his native town where his mother was buried. Then his father, who in the meantime had given him only the most meager and grudging help, made some sort of apology. He had, he said, undervalued his son's dreams and verses.

Yet when the latter shortly afterwards married, at a place some distance away, the father was angry with him and seems to have refused to recognize the wife, and though the young man was notoriously badly off he refused to give him any more money. The marriage had taken place in May; in June occurred the dream which foretold the father's death, and in September he died.

In the book which years afterward the son dedicated to his father's memory, the prophetic dream and the hallucination of the cigarette smell are represented as mystical phenomena. His feeling is that of awe rather than distress; there is at first no word of remorse. The prosaic analyst is impelled to seek a rationalistic explanation of those dreams, by no means rare, which announce the death of near relatives; and in accordance with his experience he looks for the unconscious *death wish* of the dreamer.[4]

As the son wandered about from place to place devoting himself to the art of poetry, he had at last freed himself from the passive-feminine attitude to his father, and having become able to love, he married the woman of his choice. He dared not, however, introduce her to his father, and could not go back to his native town where his beloved mother was buried. Indeed, it was just at this time that his father showed himself relentless and refused to give a single penny to the young couple, who had no resources whatever, with the result that they were in the direst need. By the process of regression the son found in his infantile hatred of the man who forbade his dreams and disturbed his love reinforcement for his unconscious death wishes, for only on his father's death could he inherit means of livelihood and be free to visit his beloved home.

That in spite of, and side by side with, all his love for his father there was even in quite early days a strong feeling of opposition to him is clear from the poet's words: as a boy "I found life difficult when I had to be my father's companion. My mother never used to speak of rules; my father on the other hand seemed to me the embodiment of his continual commands." And in another passage: "Once more I felt in my heart that there was a wide gulf between us, and I was silent, marveling that there should be no bridge between father and son, between spirit and spirit."

---

[4] Cf. Freud, *Interpretation of Dreams*, tr. by James Strachey (New York: Basic Books, 1955).

When we sum up this analysis of the poet's mind it suggests to us that the telepathic news which the son received of his dying father is not to be explained by the theory of mental "emanations" but that its origin is to be sought only in the son's unconscious mind. Even as a boy his feelings toward his harsh father were ambivalent, i.e., oscillating between love and hate. Thus, when he had just received news of his aged father's illness, at a time when through that father's fault he was in a condition of dire poverty, and more, had brought a young and dearly loved wife to share that poverty, the death wishes could be revived in his unconscious mind.

So in this second instance of clairvoyance too we find the influence of evil unconscious impulses, whose existence the son would at the time, if he had been questioned, no doubt have denied in horror. All that he was conscious of was that for some time past he had fallen a victim to the fascination of occultism, and that in dreams and at other times the thought of his father constantly occurred to him, once in the unusual form of an hallucination of the smell of his father's tobacco.

Apart from external influences, the helplessness and hopelessness of the poet would seem to be the precipitating cause of his regression to mysticism, to ideas of supernatural prevision and similar powers and of the omnipotence of thought characteristic of occultism. It reminds us of the way in which people say: "Nothing but a miracle can help me now."

That in dreams evil unconscious wishes, and especially death wishes, come to the surface is to the psychoanalyst a commonplace. The remembrance of a smell characteristic of some particular person, occurring with the vividness of an hallucination, is however something unusual and still

demands explanation. Probably the only explanation necessary lies in the intensity of the affect investing the whole
subject in the son's mind; in combination with his tendency
to visual daydreams, to clear memories and to poetic fantasies. We must remember too that his brother died a victim to delusions of persecution, a form of insanity which, as
is well-known, is also characterized by hallucinations.

Those versed in psychoanalysis will moreover recognize
that the attitude of the son who was receiving his father's
influence from a distance in this way was as it were a
passive, or, if you will, a feminine one toward the father.
An insane patient in a similar relation of dependence would
have an hallucination of being impregnated by the father,
as we know from many cases of paranoia. This "clairvoyant" period in the poet's life might be construed as a partial
regression to his attitude to his father in childhood and at
the same time as a regression to narcissism and inherited
sadism.

The assumption that intimations of the death of others
have their origin in death wishes is sufficiently well borne
out by the son's feelings of guilt after the event took place,
which appear as the autobiography proceeds. In this work,
Gedankengut aus meinen Wanderjahren [*Some Thoughts
from My Travel Years*], the poet betrays profound remorse
in connection with his father's death, because when the
news reached him he heaved a "sigh of relief" which, however, at the moment he "was not willing to admit consciously to himself." "For," he goes on, "it struck me as
ugly and ignoble that the death of my old father, whom I
loved so tenderly, should in my distressed circumstances
make me heave a sigh of relief." It was only when he came
into his father's money that he was delivered from actual
hunger and enabled to go on living. "In the frantic mockery

to which I then gave way at the thought of such a tragic situation, inheritance seemed to me synonymous with cannibalism." A skeptic might still ask how we are to account for the fact that, in the intimation of death, September was named correctly as the date of its occurrence, and that the tobacco hallucination synchronized "exactly" with the actual death. Here I would reply that we have no exact proof of the coincidence in time, that details are lacking; and further I assume that if the father had not died on that particular day of that particular month both hallucination and dream would have been forgotten, instead of proudly registered by the narcissism of the poet. At such times of mental agitation, moreover, errors and unconscious falsifications of memory are by no means uncommon.

The unscientific, unpsychological reader with a predilection for the mystical, who moves in circles where occultism and theosophy are practised and has his own part to play in them, as a "member" or even "on the committee"—this type of reader, especially if he is not restrained by any sort of scientific training, will of course reject the explanation just given. He will prefer lightheartedly to assume "some sort of wireless telegraphy," instruments keyed to the same pitch, and will quote from the special literature of the subject, etc. Why should it not be possible for telepathic influence of this sort to radiate from Würzburg to Paris? True, in other cases the chief stress is laid on the harmony existing between the two minds; it is supposed to be love which so intensifies the operation of obscure forces. Whereas in this case the father was angry with the son and wished him *not to have* any news!

Now whose voice are we to suppose it was which audibly foretold the death: "In September your father will die"? One thing the poet himself has told us—that since the break with his father, characteristically enough, he had ceased to believe in a personal God.[5] From whom did the smell of tobacco emanate? Are we to imagine that the father was smoking, mortally ill as he was? Such credulity and foolishness as this can be tolerated only where a poet's fantasy is concerned.

This intimation of the death is indeed the conscious motive of the whole *expectation* of its happening. Dauthendey started out of his sleep and heard the voice. Obviously it was an inner voice breaking in upon his sleep and accompanied by so strong an affect that the dream work could not be carried through. According to Freud, dreams are "The abolition of sleep destroying (mental) stimuli by means of hallucinatory gratification." In this case the mental stimulus was too great and sleep was destroyed; the dream turned into an audible intimation. Mental experiences of this sort which cannot be reduced to the form of dreams are also seen giving rise to many profound and lasting changes in personality; they lie at the root of religious conversions[6] and mental disorder.

Freud throws a considerable degree of light also on the genesis of hallucinations. At the moment of waking the faculty of testing reality is obviously not always functioning with sufficient accuracy to enable us to distinguish

<hr>

[5] Cf. Hitschmann. "Ein Dichter und sein Vater," *Imago*, IV (1915). By an oversight no reference was made to this work in the report on the advances in psychoanalysis between 1914 and 1919, published in the *Internationale Zeitschrift für Psychoanalyse*, or in the similar reports on *Religionswissenschaft* and *Mystik und Okkultismus*.

[6] Cf. Hitschmann, "Swedenborg's Paranoia," *Great Men*, Ed. by Sydney Margolin (New York: International Universities Press, 1956), and "Ein Dichter und sein Vater," quoted above; also, William James, *Varieties of Religious Experience* (New York: Mentor, New American Library, n.d.).

whether a psychic excitation proceeds from within (from memory) or from without (from perception). Thus the son mistook the inner voice, which predicted his father's death (of such urgent necessity to himself) as about to take place a few months later, and took it to be an outer, mystical voice, absolving him completely from his feelings of guilt. We can readily understand that in consequence his feeling was one of awe only and was without any sort of distress.

The tendency of artists toward mysticism deserves to be examined separately; the most obvious explanation is to be found in the peculiar urgency of the play of forces belonging to the repressed material in the unconscious, pressing in the direction of production. To quote a pregnant remark made by our poet, "That which I wished for in the profoundest depths of my subconsciousness always came to pass of its own accord in my life." This amounts to an indirect admission of the death wish and confirms our interpretation of the telepathic intimations he received: in his unconscious mind he had put his father to death.

VI

Clairvoyance and telepathy in the cases considered are based not on mystical or unknown physical forces, but on the psychology of the unconscious

Spontaneous clairvoyance is often (or invariably?) a purely mental subjective phenomenon. It occurs as an acute psychic phenomenon as a result of a congenital disposition in the subject, reinforced by childhood experiences, or sometimes merely through the stress of a particular situation. Forbidden wishes which have undergone repression force their way into consciousness, but reach it only in a disguised form—by which all responsibility on the part of the subject is repudiated—namely, in that of a "mystical experience" projected outwards. Contributing factors are intellectual narcissism, i.e., the craving to possess omnipotence of thought or to regard oneself as singled out for peculiar distinction by forces from the "other side." To these transitory general conditions we must add defective capacity for testing reality, while the tendency to regard oneself as specially chosen for clairvoyance and the like inhibits subsequent examination of the facts in order to establish the exact actual data. Regression to the infantile development of personality and to the level of narcissism, which is associated with the magical power of thought, causes the mind of the clairvoyant to approximate to that of primitive peoples; a weakness of intellect, affectively conditioned and with a particular bias, makes him cling to the mystical interpretation of the "experience."

Such phenomena are allied with those of dreams, tendentious wit, prophecy, conversion, etc.

Like every form of superstition clairvoyance is largely made up of an expectation of evil and, again like all superstition, has its origin in suppressed hostile and cruel impulses. In both our instances it is especially plain that the telepathic perception represents, so to speak, a psychic prothesis, a stretched out arm, which reaches out mystically toward that which is far off and cannot be approached in actuality by physical means.

Because the clairvoyant knows nothing of the motivation of his own experiences in clairvoyance, and *because* the fact of this motivation presses for recognition in him, he is obliged by a process of displacement to locate it in the outside world and to postulate supernatural forces. The assumption of the existence of mystical forces is simply psychology projected into the outer world. The endopsychic perception, the obscure apprehension of the unconscious, is reflected in the creation of transcendental forces and realities which science has to reconvert into the psychology of the unconscious.[7]

Thus, on the basis of psychoanalytical knowledge, we can explain the phenomena of clairvoyance and telepathy without finding ourselves forced to make any radical alterations in the present-day position in psychology and the natural sciences. I would repeat here my challenge of 1910,[8] that in cases of analogous telesthesia the percipient should be subjected to a psychoanalysis. This method should be used in investigating the results of automatic writing, the observations of naive participators in spiritistic séances, and so-called veridical dreams. Freud has applied his method with reference to apparently telepathic dreams[9] without deciding either for or against the reality of telepathy in the occult sense. Only by taking a leaf out of his book shall we solve the riddle.

---

[7] Cf. Freud, *Psychopathology of Everyday Life,* tr. by A. A. Brill (New York: Penguin Books, 1939).

[8] Hitschmann, "Zur Kritik des Hellsehens," *Rundschau* (Wiener Klin, 1910).

[9] Freud, "Dreams and Telepathy," *International Journal of Psycho-Analysis,* III, 283.

This paper was first given as a lecture in the Volksbild-unghaus "Urania" in Vienna in 1921. It appeared as "Telepathie und Psychoanalyse" in *Imago*, Vol. IX, 1923, and the version included here was published, in English, in the *International Journal of Psycho-Analysis*, Vol. V, 1924. The translator is unknown.

Eduard Hitschmann, who belonged to the so-called "Wednesday Evening Club" in the early days of psycho-analysis in Vienna, became well-known for his psycho-analytic interpretations of literary figures. He made extensive studies of Goethe and Swedenborg.

On dreams of flying

Paul Federn

FREUD: But why do so many people dream that they are able to fly? Psychoanalysis answers this question by stating that to fly or to be a bird in a dream is only the disguise for another wish, at the recognition of which one can arrive via more than one linguistic or objective bridge. When the inquisitive child is told that a big bird, such as the stork, brings little babies, when the ancients have equipped the phallus with wings, when the vernacular designation of the sexual activity of man is in German the expression "to bird" (*vögeln*), when the male member is directly called *l'uccello* (bird) by the Italians—all these facts are but a small fragment of the large mass of material which teaches us that the wish to be able to fly signifies in the dream neither more nor less than the longing to be capable of sexual accomplishment.[1] This is an early infantile wish.[2]

FEDERN: No type of dream presents such a challenge to the inquiry of the psychologist, or gives him such cause to ponder, as does the dream of flying. Even the dreamer

---

[1] According to the investigations of Paul Federn (1914), and of Mourly Vold (1912), a Norwegian investigator whose work lies outside the field of psychoanalysis.

[2] Freud, *Leonardo da Vinci: A Psychosexual Study of an Infantile Reminiscence*, tr. by A. A. Brill (New York: Moffat, Yard & Co., 1932), pp. 107–108.

marvels at the wonderful art, sometimes to the accompaniment of the feeling of having rediscovered a long lost ability, of a wish to preserve it now forever and to teach it to others, and of the feeling, often, that onlookers marvel at this wonderful performance of which they themselves are incapable. Even after waking, there frequently remains a feeling of pride which only gradually gives way to the realization that this goal attained through the dream, this fulfillment—which seemed so certainly achieved—of a universal wish of mankind, has faded into nothingness. But in many persons who often and throughout their lives have dreams of flying there persists a memory of a blissful inflating of the ego which carries over with a mood of happiness into the waking state, and which despite the voice of criticism repeatedly makes us believe in wonder in the field of the psychological.[3] This subject of the dream of flying is a theme of affective interest, and all the resistance encountered by the findings of Freud with regard to unconscious sexual wishes comes to the fore if one brings forward the sexual causation of dreams of flying. It is on this account that it seems to me desirable to discuss briefly the manifold sources and the mechanism of dreams of flying, and to speak in this connection of the conversion symptoms belonging to this typical dream sensation.

We wish to examine separately the question of sources and of mechanism, and we shall not be surprised to discover many and varied sources of the sensation of flying. The mechanism by which these manifold dream thoughts eventually result in the same sensation must be fundamentally

---

[3] In the appendix to his translation of Havelock Ellis' *The World of Dreams*, Kurella has very creditably collected and discussed the historical and mythological material bearing upon the significance of flying dreams for the belief in the soul and in transmigration.

the same, in so far as the sensations of flying are the same. We know, however, that the quality of the sensation of flying itself may vary considerably in the same dreamer; usually each variant is known to the dreamer. Still more varied is the method of flight in the dreams of different people. For full clarification we should therefore establish the type of regression in each variety of flying. This is possible up to a certain point. In investigating the sensation of flying we come to the gratifying conclusion that nearly all the explanations so far discovered by science are based on correct observations and are useful in so far as they reveal dream sources of the sensation or its variations or individual mechanisms of regression. A contradiction between the customary explanations and the theory of Freud based on analysis is due to faulty formulation of the problem. In addition to Freud's discovery *that the latent dream content of dreams of flying is usually a sexual one,* there is room for other dream sources, and particularly for elucidation of the psychic structure by means of which a dream thought appearing to the conscious mind so very disparate can achieve such enigmatic regressive representation. In *Interpretation of Dreams* Freud has rightly attacked the notion that observations of sensations, persisting on waking, which yield a clue to the material represented in the dream could make superfluous the question of the unconscious source of the dream and of its meaning. The fact for example that the movement of the chest can be apprehended by self-observation as a remnant of the sensation of flying will appear a sufficient explanation only to those who see in dreams nothing more than an expression of fortuitous and dissociated waking psychic elements. But those who have learned to accept Freud's psychic determinism of all psychic processes as a scientific principle will recognize in the question of unconscious dream sources the problem of the specific determination of this particular dream. The various processes which are registered in the dream as the sensation of flying are of etiological significance, then, only if they are pathologically exaggerated. In such case the affected organ may somatically facilitate the inception of the dream sensation. The sensation of flying can occur, however, without demonstrable somatic stimulus and on a purely psychogenic basis. . . .

To discuss first the sexual root of dreams of flying: this has been communicated by Freud in his *Interpretation of Dreams*, and has since been confirmed by other analysts. His formulation received another, and literary, confirmation at the hands of Mourly Vold[4] of whose work its editor, O. Klemm, promises in the preface that "with its plain setting forth of empirical material and its carefully considered ventures in interpretation, it will retain a permanent place. . . ." Vold states that if (a) tactile sensibility is inoperative, (b) a light and pleasant breath is exhaled, and, at times, (c) muscular contractions are present, then "a slight sexual vibration of the muscles of the torso—or perhaps of the whole body—releases sentimental sensations of motion and ideas which . . . assume the form of dreams of floating. . . . *The force acting from the torso itself is clearly of a sexual nature.*" In Latin he adds that this type of dream occurs in connection with a complete or beginning erection, or in very rare cases with an actual nocturnal emission.

These statements are in complete accord with the psychoanalytic experiences I am going to report, if we disregard the "vibration of the torso." It is almost amusing to see how bitter a resistance opposes the discoveries of Freud,

---

[4] "Über den Traum," *Experimental-psychologische Untersuchungen von D. I. Mourly Vold* (Leipzig, 1912).

in that an author, at the very moment when with many apologies he reports the sexual etiology of certain dreams—the very thing for which Freud was always reproached—can completely forget that Freud explicitly pointed this out. Mourly Vold says, namely, that "it is rather a matter for surprise that this motive has not been emphasized by the dream psychologists."

I myself communicated this specific etiology to the Psycho-Analytic Association four years ago—this on the basis of statements with regard to waking from dreams of flying. Professor Freud has included this communication in the latest edition of *Interpretation of Dreams*:[5] "Dr. Paul Federn (Vienna) has propounded the fascinating suggestion that a great many dreams of flying are dreams of erection, since the remarkable phenomenon of erection, which constantly occupies the human fantasy, cannot fail to be impressive as an apparent suspension of the laws of gravity (cf. the winged phalli of the ancients)." I suspect therefore that it is the physical process in the penis which finds its representation in the dream in flying. We are well acquainted with the fact that sexual processes achieve symbolic representation in most manifold forms, so that characteristically only a single feature or a single detail of the sexual activity or of the sexual organs is represented. Generally, in these representations, an object symbol corresponds to a given object, a symbolic process to an event or occurrence; one must distinguish, for example, between the erected penis and the process of erection as a dream source. . . .

Every analysis of a dream of flying discloses also motives other than sexual ones, although usually closely connected

---

[5] Freud, *Interpretation of Dreams*, tr. by James Strachey (New York: Basic Books, 1955), p. 394.

with the latter. Thus one cannot fundamentally separate exhibitionism, vanity and ambition. One can find as the dream source, in particular, the wish to surpass (*ein Überflügeln wollen*—Artemidorus), a wish to disregard certain persons, the wish to look down upon them (Freud, Stekel, Adler). The significance of the wish to travel, as emphasized by Ernest Jones, is on the one hand closely related to the sexual significance of traveling, to the erotic *Wanderlust* of adolescence especially, and on the other to death wishes, as already stated by Freud, confirmed a number of times by Stekel, and considered of importance by Jones himself. All these dream sources which I mention only in summary combine to constitute a multiple determinant of the dream of flying. The most important and the most frequent source, however, is erection. This is perceived by the infantile psyche—also biogenetically—as flying. The corresponding normal sensory perception, not as magnified dreamwise, belongs in the category of vertigo. Thus can be demonstrated the beginning of the psychic alteration, namely the conception of erection as the desire to fly, and the end, the regression to the sense organ. The mechanisms which in the individual case can make this potential representation into an actual one are clear only in so far as an acute increase in masculine libido may give rise to a dream of flying. It remains a question, however, how far we have to do with a historical and how far with a purely psychological regression. With the answer to this question are connected important problems relating to the psychology of the neuroses. . . .

We may assume with certainty that sexual sources gave rise to the sensation of flying, in opposition to the resistance of the censorship, that regression persisted for a brief time into the period of waking, and that the conscious psyche became aware of it in the form of vertigo as the corresponding process in the equilibratory apparatus. Since this sensation of dizziness was the same as during the neurosis, the indication is that the regression, otherwise present only in the dream, occurred during the neurosis in the waking state also. While therefore in the healthy psyche flying exists only as a potentiality, an idea capable of entering consciousness and without sexual accentuation—in the neurosis this idea is enormously intensified, constantly stimulating the sensory sphere and bringing about regression. If we remember that motives of ambition may also be the basis for the sensation of flying, we shall not be surprised to find that neurotic vertigo is so often associated with the anxiety of ambition. The relationship between sexuality and ambition, on the one hand, and neurotic vertigo on the other does not require demonstration solely through ideas of flying. We know that various bodily movements which cause vertigo through regression occur as sexual symbols. I hope I have been able to show by means of this specific example the significance of typical dream sensations for the understanding of conversion symptoms.

This paper first appeared in *Jahrbuch für Psychoanalyse*, Vol. VI, 1914, as part of an article entitled "Über zwei typische Traumsensationen." It was later printed in the *International Journal of Psycho-Analysis* for 1916; the translator is unknown. It was included in the *Psychoanalytic Reader*, Vol. I, edited by Robert Fliess (New York: International Universities Press, 1948).

Paul Federn was another of the pioneers of Viennese psychoanalysis. He attended the Wednesday evening sessions of Freud's circle, and wrote prolifically.

On the theory of analysis of children

Anna Freud

Ladies and Gentlemen:

Three papers on the subject of analyzing children are being read before you at this Congress—instead of only one, which has hitherto been the order of the day—and this alone illustrates the importance that the subject has acquired in the eyes of the International Association during the last few years. I think that the reason for this accession of interest in child analysis lies in the threefold contribution it can make to our psychoanalytical knowledge. It gives us welcome confirmations of those conceptions of the mental life of children which, in the course of years, have been deduced by psychoanalytical theory from the analyses of adults. Secondly, as Mrs. Klein's paper has just demonstrated, the direct observation thus employed leads us to fresh conclusions and supplementary conceptions, and, finally, it serves as a point of transition to a field of applied analysis which, as many hold, will in the future be one of the most important. I refer to pedagogy.

Thus, strong in the sense of its threefold usefulness, child analysis ventures to claim liberty and independence in various directions. It demands a new technique. This is will-

ingly conceded: even the most conservative person realizes
without difficulty that a difference in the object with which
one is dealing demands different methods of approach.
Thus Melanie Klein has evolved the play technique for
the analysis of little children, and, later, I myself put forward suggestions for the analysis of children in the latency
period. But certain advocates of child analysis (myself
amongst them) go further still. They begin to ponder the
question whether the processes in child analysis are always
wholly identical, from the theoretical standpoint, with
those in the analysis of adults, and whether the aims and
objects of the two forms of treatment are exactly the
same. The people who follow this line of thought hold that
those who analyze children should possess not only the
correct analytical training and mental attitude but something further: something which is called for by the idiosyn-
crasies of childhood, namely, the training and the mental
attitude of the pedagogue. I think we ought not to be dis-
mayed by this word or to conclude offhand that to combine the two attitudes is somehow derogatory to analysis.
It is worth-while to take some concrete examples and see
whether the demand for such a combination can at all be
justified or whether the right thing is to reject it as il-
legitimate.

The first example I shall select for this purpose is a
fragment from the analysis of an eleven-year-old boy.
When he first came for treatment his disposition was of the
feminine-masochistic type, his original object-relation with
his mother being wholly overlaid by his identification of
himself with her. His original masculine aggressive tendencies only occasionally found a vent in hostile behavior to
his brothers and sisters and isolated asocial acts; these were
succeeded by violent outbreaks of remorse and by depression of spirits. I am now quoting from a period in his

analysis in which his mind was occupied with countless thoughts, fantasies and dreams about death, or, more precisely, about killing.

Just at this time a very intimate friend of his mother's was seriously ill, and his mother was informed by telegram of her friend's danger. The patient seized upon this opportunity to weave fantasies in this connection. He fantasied that another telegram came saying: "She is dead." His mother was much grieved. Then yet another telegram arrived saying that it was a mistake, the friend was alive again. His mother rejoiced. Then, in his fantasy, he caused telegrams to arrive in rapid succession—one saying that the friend was dead and the next that she had come to life again. The whole fantasy ended with the news that it was all a joke which had been played on his mother. It is not difficult to interpret the fantasy. We see clearly the boy's ambivalence, his desire to kill the person whom his mother loved and his inability actually to carry his purpose through.

Soon after this he told me of the following obsessive act. When he was sitting in the w.c. he felt impelled to touch a knob on the wall on one side three times with his hand and immediately afterwards to do the same to a knob on the other side. At first this action seemed incomprehensible, but a few days later we found the explanation in a fantasy which he recounted in another connection. He imagined God as an old man sitting on a great throne in the courts of Heaven. To the right and left of Him were knobs or switches on the wall. If he pressed a knob on one side, some human being died; if he pressed one on the other side a child was born into the world. I think, if we compare the boy's obsessive action with this daydream, it will be superfluous to interpret it further. The number three is probably explained by the number of the other children in the family.

Soon after this, a friend of the family, the father of one

of his playfellows and a man whom his mother knew very intimately, fell ill. On the way to his analysis the patient heard the telephone bell ring, and, while with me, he made up the following fantasy: His mother had been sent for to the sick man's house. She went in, entered the sickroom, went up to the bed and tried to speak to her friend, the patient. But he did not answer, and then she saw that he was dead. It was a great shock to her. At that moment the dead man's little son came in. She called him and said: "Come and look, your father is dead." The boy went up to the bed and spoke to his father, whereupon the father came to life and answered him. The child then turned to my patient's mother and said: "What do you mean? He is *alive*." The mother then spoke to the man again; once more he did not reply, for he was dead. But when the little boy came in again and spoke to him, the father came to life.

I have recounted this fantasy in such detail because it is so instructive and transparent, and contains in itself the interpretation of the two previously quoted. We see that the father is dead as far as his relation to the mother is concerned; as soon as it is a question of himself and his son, he is alive. In the earlier fantasies the ambivalent feelings to the same person—the desire to kill and the opposite desire to keep alive or to bring back to life—were simply separated into two different actions, canceling one another. This last fantasy however, contains in addition a specification of the person threatened (on the one hand as husband and on the other as father), and here we have the historic explanation of the boy's twofold attitude. Obviously the two tendencies originate in different phases of his development. The death wish against the father as the rival for the mother's love springs from the normal Œdipus phase with the positive object love (since repressed) to the mother. Here his masculine aggressive impulses are directed against the father, who is to be killed to leave the way clear for the boy himself. But the other tendency—the desire to keep the father for himself—originates on the one hand in the early period, when the son's attitude to the father was one of pure admiration and love, undisturbed by the rivalry connected with the Œdipus complex, and on the other (and this is the more important here) belongs to the phase of identification with the mother which has succeeded to the normal Œdipus attitude. Out of dread of the castration with which he is menaced by the father the boy has renounced his love for his mother and let himself be forced into the feminine position. Here he is forced to try to keep his father as the object of his homosexual love.

It is tempting to go on and describe the transition by which this boy passed from the desire to kill to a dread of death which awoke in him at night, and hence to gain access to the complicated structure of this neurosis of the latency period. But you know that that is not part of my purpose here. I have cited this fragment simply in order that you may confirm my impression that this part of the analysis of a child differs in no way from that of an adult. What we have to do is to free some of his masculine aggression and his object love for his mother from repression and from being buried beneath his now feminine-masochistic character and his identification of himself with his mother. The conflict which we come upon here is an inner one. Even if originally dread of his real father in the outside world impelled him to make the repression, its success now depends on forces within himself. The father has been internalized, and the superego has become the representative of his power; the boy's dread of him is experienced as dread of castration. Outbreaks of this castration anxiety hinder every step which the analysis endeavors to make toward bringing the repressed Œdipus tendencies into consciousness. Only the slow analytical dissection of the superego, in historical sequence, makes it possible for my work of liberation to advance. Thus you see that, as far as this part of the task is concerned, the work and the attitude of the analyst are purely analytical. There is no place here for the introduction of educational methods.

Now let me give you an example where the opposite is the case. It is taken from the analysis of a little girl of six, part of which I have already published elsewhere for a different purpose. Here again (as always) it is a question of the impulses arising out of the Œdipus complex and once more the attitude toward killing comes in. The analysis showed that the little girl had passed through an early phase of passionate love for her father and, in the usual way, had been disappointed by him through the birth of younger brothers and sisters. Her reaction to this disappointment was extraordinarily strong. Having barely attained to the genital phase, she abandoned it and regressed completely to the level of anal sadism. She turned her hostile impulses against the newly arrived younger children. She attempted to retain her father, from whom her love had almost entirely withdrawn itself, by incorporation if in no other way. But her efforts to feel herself a male came to grief in competition with an elder brother, for she realized that he was physically better equipped in this direction than she herself. The result was intense hostility to her mother: hate, first, because she had taken the father away from herself; secondly, because she had not made her herself a boy; and, finally, because the mother had borne the brothers and sisters whom she herself would have liked to bring into the world. But at this point—when my patient was about four years old—something of importance happened. She realized dimly that because of her hate reaction she was on the way to losing the happy relation with her mother, whom she had loved dearly, in spite of all, from her earliest infancy. And in order not to lose this love for her mother and, still more, her mother's love for her, without which she could not live, she made a tremendous effort to become "good." Suddenly and, as it were, at a single blow she dissociated herself from all this hatred and with it from her whole sexual life, consisting of anal and sadistic behavior and fantasies. She opposed it to her own personality as something alien, no longer part of herself, something which came from "the devil." There was not much left: a tiny, cramped personality, whose emotional life was not wholly her own to control and whose very considerable intelligence and energy were devoted to keeping "the devil" in his state of forcible repression. In her relations with the outside world she was merely apathetic, while the lukewarm feelings of tenderness and affection for her mother were not strong enough to bear the slightest strain. And more than this: the dissociation which she had striven to accomplish could not be permanently maintained in spite of her great expenditure of effort. At times "the devil" would get the better of her for a short while and she fell into states in which without any adequate external cause she would throw herself on the ground and scream in a way which in the old days would certainly have been described as "possession." Or she would suddenly surrender herself to the other side of her nature and luxuriate with the utmost enjoyment in sadistic fantasies, as, for example, that she roamed through her parents' house from attic to cellar, breaking up all the furniture and every object she came across and throwing them out of the window, and without more ado cutting off the heads of all the people she met. Such occasions of being overmastered by the devil were invariably followed by anxiety and remorse. But there was another, still more dangerous way in which the dissociated evil tendencies used to break out. "The devil" loved feces and dirt: she herself began gradually to develop a peculiar anxiety in regard to habits of cleanliness. "The devil" particularly enjoyed cutting off people's heads, so at certain times she was compelled to creep to the beds of her brothers and sisters early in the morning and see that they were still all alive. "The devil" took a delight in energetically transgressing every human commandment, and so the child began to suffer from a dread of earthquakes, at night before she went to sleep, because someone had told her that an earthquake was the most terrific punishment which God was wont to inflict on human beings. Thus her daily life was in all sorts of ways made up of actions which either were substitutes for those of the dissociated evil nature or represented her remorse and endeavors to atone. So we may say that her magnificently conceived attempt to retain her mother's love and to conform to social requirements and become "good" had failed miserably. The only result was an obsessional neurosis.

Now I did not enlist your interest in this infantile neurosis because of its fine structure and the fact that the symptoms were defined with a clearness unusual in so young a patient. My reason for describing it to you was a peculiar circumstance which struck me while I was treating the child.

In the case of the eleven-year-old boy which I described before you will remember that the motive factor in the repression was the dread of castration by the father. Naturally, the resistance which I observed in the analysis was this same castration anxiety. But in the case of the little girl it was different. The repression, or rather the cleavage, in the childish personality was brought about under the stress of a dread of loss of love. According to our notions, the anxiety must have been very intense to be able so to disturb the child's whole life. But in the analysis this very anxiety could hardly be detected as a serious resistance. Finding that my interest remained uniformly friendly, the little patient began to display to me her bad side quite calmly and frankly. You will reply that that is not very surprising. I know that we often meet with adult patients who anxiously and with an uneasy conscience keep their symptoms a secret from the whole world and begin to expose them only in the secure atmosphere of analysis with its freedom from criticism. Often, indeed, it is only then that they come to know what they really are. But this applies only to their describing of their symptoms: the analyst's friendly interest and the absence of the criticism the patients anticipate never actually bring about a transformation in the symptoms. But that was exactly what happened in the case of this little girl. When she found that not only was I interested and refrained from condemning her, but that also less strict demands were made upon her at home, her anxiety was transformed under my very eyes in analysis into the wish which it concealed, while the reaction formation turned into the instinct which it was designed to keep at bay and the precautionary measure into the threat to kill which lay behind it. But of the dread of loss of love, which surely should have broken out violently in opposition to such a reversal, there was scarcely a sign. The resistance was weaker on this side than on any other. It was as though the little girl said to herself: "If you don't think it so very bad, then I don't either." And, as her demands upon herself became less exacting, gradually, as the analysis went on, she incorporated once more within herself all the tendencies which she had rejected at the cost of so much energy—her incestuous love for her father, her desire to be a boy, her death wishes against her brothers and sisters and the recognition of her infantile sexuality. The only check was a temporary one due to the sole serious resistance when she came to what seemed the worst of all: the recognition of the direct death wish against her mother.

Now this is not the behavior which we are accustomed to see in the normal superego. Surely, adult neurotics teach us how impervious to reason that superego is, how obstinately it opposes every attempt at influence from without and how it refuses to modify its demands until it has been dissected in the analysis in historical sequence and every individual command and prohibition has been traced to someone who was important and beloved by the patient in childhood.

Ladies and gentlemen, I think that here we have lighted on the most important, fundamental difference beween the analysis of adults and that of children. In the analysis of the adult we are at a point where the superego has already established its independence—an independence which is unshakable by any influence from the outside world. Here the only thing for us to do is to bring into consciousness, and thus raise to the same level, all the tendencies belonging to the id, the ego and the superego respectively which have played a part in the neurotic conflict. On this new level of consciousness the battle may be fought out in a new way and be brought to a different issue. But child analysis must include all those cases in which the superego has as yet not reached any true independence. Only too clearly it strives to please its taskmasters, the child's parents and others responsible for his training, and in its demands it reflects every oscillation in the relation to these beloved persons and all the changes in their own views. Here, as in the analysis of adults, we work on purely analytical lines in so far as our object is to free from the unconscious those parts of the id and the ego which have already been repressed. But our work in relation to the childish superego is twofold: on the one hand, as analysts, in so far as the superego has already attained to independence, we have to assist in the dissection of the material from within, following the historical sequence, but, in addition to this, we have to use our influence from without in an educational manner by changing the child's relation to those who are bringing him up, by providing him with new ideas and by revising the demands which the outside world is making upon him.

Let us go back once more to my little girl patient. If she had not come for treatment at the age of six probably her infantile neurosis would, like so many others, have spontaneously cleared up. In that case it is certain that it would have bequeathed to her a strict superego which would have made implacable demands on the ego and have opposed any subsequent analysis in the form of a resistance hard to overcome. But my view is that this strict superego appears at the end and not at the beginning of children's neuroses.

In order to illustrate this point I would refer you to a case recently described by Dr. M. W. Wulff.[1] He gives an account of anxiety attacks of the nature of phobias in a baby girl of eighteen months. It is plain that the parents of this child had exacted habits of cleanliness from her too early. The baby was unable to obey them and began to be mentally disturbed and afraid that they might send her away. Her anxiety reached the pitch of actual attacks when it was dark or when she heard strange noises, e.g., if some-

[1] *International Journal of Psycho-Analysis*, Vol. IX, Part 3 (1928).

one knocked at the door. She asked over and over again if she were good and begged them not to send her away. The parents, much concerned, consulted Dr. Wulff.

I think that the interesting thing about this early symptom is that the baby's anxiety, which Dr. Wulff immediately diagnosed as dread of the loss of love, could in no way be differentiated from the anxiety of conscience in an adult neurotic. Now, in this case, are we to believe that conscience (i.e. the superego) had developed so early? Dr. Wulff explained to the parents that the little girl obviously was for some reason or other unequal to the demand for cleanliness, and he advised them to defer her training in this respect for a time. The parents had sufficient understanding to agree. They explained to the child that they loved her even when she wetted herself, and, whenever this happened, they repeatedly tried to calm her with assurances of their love. The success of this experiment was, as Dr. Wulff tells us, striking. After a few days the child was calm and free from anxiety.

Naturally treatment of this sort is applicable but rarely, and only with very little children. I do not want you to receive the impression that I am recommending it as the only possible course. But here Dr. Wulff was making the patient's cure the test of his treatment, and this is the only test which can reveal to us what is the play of forces which is giving rise to anxiety. If the child had really fallen ill because of the excessive demands of her own superego, her parents' reassurances could not have had any influence at all on her symptoms. But if the cause of her anxiety was a real fear of the displeasure of her parents as they actually existed in the outside world (and not of her imagos of them), we can easily understand her illness being cured. For Dr. Wulff had removed the cause.

Quite a number of other childish reactions can be similarly explained only by the superego's accessibility to influence in the early years of life. By the kindness of Dr. Ferenczi I have had an opportunity of seeing the notes of a mistress at one of the modern American schools, the Walden School. This mistress, who has had a psychoanalytical training, describes how neurotic children whose home standards are strict, and who come to her school while still at the kindergarten age, after a longer or shorter period of holding back in amazement, grow accustomed to the extraordinarily free atmosphere and gradually lose their neurotic symptoms, most of which are reactions to breaking the habit of onanism. We know that with an adult neurotic it would be impossible to produce a similar effect. The freer the environment into which he finds himself transplanted the greater is his dread of the instinct in question and, therewith, the more marked the accentuation of his neurotic defense reactions, i.e., his symptoms. The demands made on him by his superego are no longer susceptible to influence from his environment. A child, on the contrary, once he begins to modify his standards, is inclined rather to go a long way in this direction and allow himself more latitude than even the freest surroundings could permit him. In this respect, as in others, he cannot do without influence from others.

And now, in conclusion, let me give a very innocent example. A little time ago I had an opportunity of listening to the talk of a five-year-old boy and his mother. The child had conceived a wish for a live horse, and the mother, for good reasons, refused to give it to him. "It doesn't matter," he said, nothing daunted, "I will ask for it on my next birthday." His mother assured him that he would not have it even then. "Then I'll ask for it at Christmas," he said, "you can have anything then." "No, not even at Christmas," said his mother, trying to disillusion him. He thought for a moment. "Well, it *doesn't* matter," he said triumphantly, "I'll buy it for myself. *I* will let myself have it." You see, ladies and gentlemen, that already between his inner permission and the prohibition imposed from without there arises the conflict which may terminate in all sorts of ways: in rebellion and asocial behavior, in neurosis and, fortunately, often in health.

Now let me say just one word about the attitude of the children's analyst as an educationist. We have recognized that the forces arrayed against us in our fight to cure neurosis in children are not merely internal but also in part external. This gives us the right to require that the analyst shall understand aright the part played by the outward situation in which the child is placed, just as we require that he shall grasp the child's inner situation. But in order to fulfill this part of his task a children's analyst must have a knowledge of the theory and practice of pedagogy. This will enable him to ascertain the influences being brought to bear on the child by those who are training him, to criticize them and (if it proves necessary) to take the work of his upbringing out of their hands for the period of the analysis and to undertake it himself.

This paper was given as a lecture before the Tenth International Psycho-Analytical Congress at Innsbruck on September 3, 1927. It first appeared in the *Internationale Zeitschrift für Psychoanalyse*, Vol. XIV, 1928, and was subsequently printed in English in the *International Journal of Psycho-Analysis*, Vol. X, 1929; the translator is unknown.

Anna Freud was the only one of Freud's children to make psychoanalysis her profession. She became a pioneer in the field of child psychoanalysis.

Psychoanalysis and the concept of health

Heinz Hartmann

Perhaps it would be true to say that we attach less importance in analytical circles to differentiating between healthy and pathological behavior than is often done outside those circles. But the concepts of "health" and "illness" always exert a "latent" influence, so to say, on our analytical habits of thought and it cannot but serve a useful purpose to clarify the implications of these terms. Moreover, it would be a mistake to suppose that the subject possesses no more than a theoretical interest, that it lacks any practical significance. For, when all is said and done, it often depends upon the analytical concept of health whether we recommend a course of analytical treatment—so that the matter is important as a factor in our judgment of the indications present— or what changes we should like to see effected in a patient, or when we may consider that an analysis is ripe for termination. Differences of outlook in this sphere must ultimately lead to corresponding differences in our therapeutic technique, as was clearly foreseen by Ernest Jones[1] many years ago.

---

[1] See "The Attitude of the Psycho-Analytic Physician towards Current Conflicts," *Papers on Psycho-Analysis* (3rd ed.; London: 1916; 5th ed.; Baltimore: Williams and Wilkins, 1950).

While psychoanalysis was still in its infancy, it seemed a relatively simple matter to define mental health and mental illness. At that period we became acquainted for the first time with the conflicts which give rise to neuroses and believed that we had thereby acquired the right to differentiate beween health and illness. Subsequently the discovery was made that conflicts such as those we had come to regard as pathogenic could be shown to exist also in healthy people; it became apparent that the choice between health and illness was determined rather by temporal and quantitative factors. To a greater extent than any theoretical considerations our therapeutic experience has compelled us to recognize this truth. It has been found that our efforts have met with very variable success and we are not always able to accept the familiar explanations of the responsibility for this state of affairs. We are finally forced to the conclusion that the quantitative factor of the strength of the instincts and a quantitative factor residing in the ego function have here acquired, side by side with other factors of course, an importance of their own. Moreover, mechanisms are evidently not as such pathogenic but only in virtue of their topographical value in space and their dynamic value in action, if I may so express myself. The process of modifying the original analytical conception of health has been advanced a stage further by the contributions to the psychology of the ego which have now been in the forefront of psychoanalytical interest for nearly twenty years. But the more we begin to understand the ego and its maneuvers and achievements in dealing with the external world, the more do we tend to make these functions of adaptation, achievement, etc. the touchstone of the concept of health.

However, a psychoanalytical definition of health presents certain difficulties which we shall now proceed to examine. As is well known, it is never at any time an easy matter to say what we really mean by "health" and "illness" and perhaps the difficulty of differentiating between them is even greater when we are concerned with the so-called "psychological illnesses" than it is with physical maladies. Health is certainly not a purely statistical average. If it were we should have to look upon the exceptional achievements of single individuals as pathological, which would be contrary to the ordinary usage of speech; and besides this, a majority of people exhibit characteristics which are generally regarded as pathological (the example most frequently given being caries of the teeth). "Abnormal" then, in the sense of a deviation from the average, is not synonymous with "pathological."

In the conceptions of health most widely prevalent, subjective valuations play a considerable part, whether explicitly or implicitly, and that is the chief reason why such conceptions, especially when they relate to mental health and mental illness, may vary considerably at different periods and among different peoples. Here judgment is influenced by a subjective factor depending on cultural and social conditions and even personal values. Within a uniform society these judgments will exhibit a far-reaching similarity, but that does not deprive them in the least of their subjective character. "Health" is generally one expression of the idea of vital perfection; and this in itself implies the subjectivity of the judgments concerning it. A logical analysis of the concept of health (I shall barely touch upon the problem here) would have to devote especial attention to the valuations embodied in the different conceptions of health.

But these are not the only difficulties inherent in a psychoanalytical definition of health. So long as we make freedom from symptoms, for instance, the criterion of mental health, it is comparatively easy in practice to arrive at a decision. Even by this standard there exists no absolutely objective basis for our judgment; for a simple answer is not readily forthcoming to the question whether a given psychical manifestation is in the nature of a symptom or whether on the contrary it is to be regarded as an "achievement." It is often a difficult matter to decide whether the pedantry or ambition of an individual or the nature of his object choice are symptoms in a neurotic sense or character traits possessing a positive value for health. Nevertheless this standard does provide us, if not with a basis for objective judgment, at all events with a consensus of opinion which is usually sufficient for all practical purposes. But health as it is understood in psychoanalysis is something which means far more than this. In our view, freedom from symptoms is not enough for health; and we cherish higher expectations of the therapeutic effects of psychoanalysis. But over and above this, psychoanalysis has witnessed the development of a number of theoretical conceptions of health which often lay down very severe standards. We have accordingly to ask ourselves what health signifies in a psychoanalytical sense.

By way of preamble we would remark that man's relation to health and illness itself often presents features of a distinctly neurotic order. When these problems are very much in the foreground one is sometimes actually tempted to speak of a "health neurosis." This idea is made the basis of a paper recently published by Melitta Schmideberg.[2] A conspicuous characteristic in certain well-marked types is their conviction that they themselves enjoy superior health, accompanied by a compulsive urge to detect in others devi-

[2] See "After the Analysis . . . ," *Psychoanalytic Quarterly*, VII (1938).

ations, mainly of a neurotic or psychotic kind, from their ideal of health. In certain circumstances such people are capable of fulfilling a useful function in society by very reason of their particular form of neurosis, which may mark them out for the role of eternal sick nurse to their fellow men. In the simplest form of this behavior the operative mechanism is commonly projection; by constantly seeing others as patients in need of one's help one avoids recognition of one's own neurosis. In the same way Freud once expressed the opinion that many analysts probably learn to absolve themselves from personal compliance with the obligations of analysis by exacting it from others. We know too that a like tendency to overestimate the neurotic and psychotic reactions of one's fellow men belongs to the growing pains of many analysts. It is a common feature of "health neuroses" that those afflicted by them cannot allow themselves to suffer or to feel ill or depressed.[3] But a healthy person must have the capacity to suffer and to be depressed. Our clinical experience has taught us the consequences of glossing over illness and suffering, of being unable to admit to oneself the possibility of illness and suffering. It is even probable that a limited amount of suffering and illness forms an integral part of the scheme of health, as it were, or rather that health is only reached by indirect ways. We know that successful adaptation can lead to maladaptation—the development of the superego is a case in point and many other examples could be cited. But conversely, maladaptation may become successful adaptation. Typical conflicts are a part and parcel of "normal" development and disturbances in adaptation are included in its scope. We discover a similar state of affairs in relation to the therapeutic process of analysis. Here health clearly includes pathological reactions as a means toward its attainment.

[3] Cf. Schmideberg, *op. cit.*

But we must return to the concept of health and ask ourselves once more what criteria we possess in analysis for
gauging mental health and illness. I have already mentioned
that we do not identify health with freedom from symptoms. And we still find ourselves on ground which is comparatively accessible, from an empirical though not, of
course, from a prognostic point of view, if we take into
consideration the extent to which this immunity from
symptoms is durable and capable of withstanding shocks.
But the wider implications which the term health assumes
for us and what analysis aims at in this sense cannot readily
be reduced to a scientific formula. At the same time we find
a number of useful theoretical formulations concerning the
attributes of that state of health to which we are anxious to
bring our patients with the help of the methods available to
analysis. Of these the most general is Freud's "Where id
was, there shall ego be";[4] or there is Nunberg's "the energies
of the id become more mobile, the superego more tolerant,
the ego becomes more free from anxiety and its synthetic
function is restored."[5] But the distance between such necessarily schematic formulations and the measurement of
actual states of mental health, of the actual degree of
mental health enjoyed by a given individual, is far greater
than one would like to suppose. It is not at all a simple matter to bring these theoretical conceptions of health into line
with what we in actual fact call "healthy." Moreover, one
gains an impression that individual conceptions of health
differ widely among analysts themselves, varying with the
aims which each has set for himself on the basis of his views
concerning human development, and also of course with
his philosophy, political sympathies, etc. Perhaps for the

---

[4] See *New Introductory Lectures*, tr. by W. J. Sprott (New
York: W. W. Norton, 1933).
[5] See *Allgemeine Neurosenlehre* (Berlin: H. Huber, 1932).

time being it will be advisable to proceed with caution before attempting to arrive at a precise theoretical formulation of the concept of health—otherwise we shall be in danger of allowing our standards of health to become dependent on our moral preoccupations and other subjective aspirations. It is clearly essential to proceed on purely empirical lines, i.e., to examine from the point of view of their structure and development the personalities of those who are actually considered healthy instead of allowing our theoretical speculations to dictate to us what we "ought" to regard as healthy. This is precisely the attitude that psychoanalysis adopts toward the normative disciplines. It does not ask whether these norms are justified but concentrates on a totally different problem, namely that of the genesis and structure of behavior which has, in fact, for whatever reason, been assigned a place in a scale of positive and negative values. And besides, theoretical standards of health are usually too narrow in so far as they underestimate the great diversity of types which in practice pass as healthy. Needless to say analysis itself possesses criteria intended to serve as a purely practical guide, such as the tests so frequently applied of a capacity for achievement or enjoyment.

But we propose here to examine in greater detail those theoretical schemes for the classification of mental health and illness which one finds contained, either expressly or by implication, in psychoanalytical literature; and for this purpose we may ask ourselves what conceptions of health have in fact been advanced and not whether certain conceptions "ought" to be advanced. These descriptions of a healthy or "biologically adjusted" individual, if we confine ourselves entirely to their broadest general outlines, reveal a pronounced development in two directions. In neither direction, it need scarcely be said, is it merely a question of some subjective factor, some personal predilection achieving expression; they are the results of a rich harvest of clinical experience, and of much valuable experience of the analytical process of cure. These two directions emphasize as the goal of development and health on the one hand rational behavior and on the other hand instinctual life. This twofold orientation already commands our interest because it reflects the twofold origin of psychoanalysis in the history of thought—the rationalism of the Age of Enlightenment and the irrationalism of the Romantics. The circumstance that these two aspects are emphasized in Freud's work certainly reflects a genuine insight into the dualism which does in fact inform the problem. Now the analytical conceptions of health which have developed on the basis of Freud's suggestions often proceed to assign undue prominence to one of these standpoints at the expense of the other.

When one makes the mistake in analysis of contrasting the id as the biological part of the personality with the ego as its non-biological component, one naturally encourages the tendency to make "life" and "mind" into absolutes. When in addition all biological values are acknowledged as supreme, one has approached dangerously near to that malady of the times whose nature it is to worship instinct and pour scorn on reason. To be sure, these tendencies, which lead to a glorification of instinctual man and which at the present time have widely assumed a highly aggressive and political complexion, play a less conspicuous part in the literature pertaining to psychoanalysis or subject to its influence than they do elsewhere.

At the other end of the scale we find the ideal of a rational attitude, and the "perfectly rational" man is here held up as a model of health and as an ideal figure generally.

This conception of mental health deserves closer consideration. That some connection exists between reason and successful adaptation seems clear enough, but it is apparently not such a simple one as is assumed in many psychoanalytical writings. We should not take it for granted that recognition of reality is the equivalent of adaptation to reality. The most rational attitude does not necessarily constitute an optimum for the purposes of adaptation. When we say that an idea or system of ideas is "in accordance with reality," this may mean that the theoretical content of the system is true, but it can also signify that the translation of these ideas into action results in conduct appropriate to the occasion. A correct view of reality is not the sole criterion of whether a particular action is in accordance with reality. We must also reflect that a healthy ego should be able to make use of the system of rational control and at the same time take into account the fact of the irrational nature of other mental activities. (This is a part of its coordinating function.) The rational must incorporate the irrational as an element in its design. Moreover, we shall have to admit that the advance of the "rational attitude" is not an even one along a single front, as it were. One often has the impression that a partial progression in this respect may entail a partial regression in other directions. It is evidently very much the same with the process of civilization as a whole. Technical progress may very well be accompanied by mental regression or may actually bring it about by way of mass methods.[6] Here I can only present these ideas in brief outline but I have developed them at greater length elsewhere. They show us the need to revise those analytical conceptions which maintain that the individual

---

[6] See Karl Mannheim, *Man and Society in the Age of Reconstruction* (London: Kegan Paul, 1939).

who is most rational (in the ordinary sense of the word) is also psychologically the most completely healthy.

Another fundamental criterion of mental health available to psychology has a somewhat less general character, one more firmly rooted in the structural conceptions of analysis: I refer to the criterion of freedom. By freedom is meant not the philosophical problem of free will but rather freedom from anxiety and affects, or freedom to perform a task. The credit for introducing this criterion into analysis belongs to Wälder.[7] I believe that at the root of this conception there lies a well-founded idea; yet I would rather have avoided the term freedom because it is so equivocal in meaning and has been so heavily overtasked by successive philosophers. In the present context it means no more than control exercised by means of the conscious and preconscious ego and might well be replaced by that description. The mobility or plasticity of the ego is certainly one of the prerequisites of mental health, whereas a rigid ego may interfere with the process of adaptation. But we would add that a healthy ego is not only and at all times plastic. Important as is this quality, it seems to be subordinated to another of the ego's functions. A clinical example will make this clear. We are all familiar with the obsessional neurotic's fear of losing his self-control—a factor which makes it so very difficult for him to associate freely. The phenomenon which I am thinking of is even more clearly marked in those persons who, for fear of losing their ego, are unable to achieve orgasm. These pathological manifestations teach us that a healthy ego must evidently be in a position to allow some of its most essential functions, including its "freedom,"

---

[7] "The Problem of Freedom in Psycho-Analysis and the Problem of Reality-Testing," *International Journal of Psycho-Analysis,* XVII (1936).

to be put out of action occasionally, so that it may abandon itself to "compulsion" (central control). This brings us to the problem, hitherto almost entirely neglected, of a biological hierarchy of the ego's functions and to the notion of the integration of opposites, which we have already met in connection with the problem of rational conduct. I believe that these considerations relative to the mobility of the ego and the automatic disconnecting of vital ego functions have enabled us to make very considerable progress toward discovering an important condition of mental health. The threads which lead us from this point to the concept of ego strength are clearly visible. But I do not now wish to discuss this well-worn theme, although one would have to deal with it at considerable length if a systematic exposition of our subject were intended, which is not the case.

I shall now develop this critical exposition of analytical conceptions of health in a direction which will enable us to penetrate more deeply into the realm of ego theory. For obvious reasons psychoanalysis has hitherto been concerned principally with situations in which the ego finds itself in conflict with the id and the superego and, more recently, with the external world. Now one sometimes meets with the idea that the contrast between a conflict-ridden and a peaceful development can automatically be correlated with that afforded by mental health and mental illness. This is a quite mistaken view: conflicts are a part and parcel of human development, for which they provide the necessary stimulus. Nor does the distinction between healthy and pathological reactions correspond to that between behavior originating or not originating in defense. Nevertheless it is by no means an uncommon thing to discover passages in psychoanalytical literature in which it is maintained that whatever is prompted by the needs of defense, or else results from unsuccessful defense, must somehow be accounted as pathological. Yet it is perfectly clear that a measure which is successful in relation to defensive needs may be a failure from the standpoint of positive achievement, and vice versa. We are really concerned here with two distinct approaches to the classification of the same facts and not with two different sets of facts. This consideration does not invalidate our experience that pathological function offers the most fruitful approach to the problems of mental conflict. Similarly we first became familiar with the mechanisms of defense in their pathogenic aspect and it is only now that we are gradually coming to recognize the part they play in normal development. It would seem that we cannot adequately assess the positive or negative value which such processes possess for mental health so long as we only think of the problems of mental conflict and fail to consider these matters from the standpoint of adaptation as well.

Now if we examine these situations more attentively, we very often make the interesting discovery that the shortest way to reality is not always the most promising from the standpoint of adaptation. It would seem that we often learn to find our bearings in relation to reality by devious ways, and that it is inevitable and not merely "accidental" that this should be the case. There is evidently a typical sequence here, withdrawal from reality leading to an increased mastery over it. (In its essential features this pattern is already realized in the process of our thinking; the same remark applies to the activity of imagination, the avoidance of unsatisfactory situations, etc.) The theory of the neuroses has always presented the mechanism of turning away from reality solely in terms of pathological processes: but an approach from the standpoint of the problems of adaptation teaches us that such mechanisms have a positive value for health.[8]

In this connection a further problem has a claim upon our interest: I allude to the way in which we use the terms "regression" and "regressive" within the analytical system of criteria for measuring mental health. We are generally accustomed to think of regressive behavior as the antithesis of conduct adapted to reality. We are all familiar with the part which regression plays in pathogenesis and for that very reason I shall not need to consider that aspect of the problem. But in actual fact it would seem that we have to distinguish between progressive and regressive forms of adaptation. We shall have no difficulty in defining a progressive adaptation: it means an adaptation in the direction of development. But we also find instances of successful adaptation achieved by way of regression. These comprise many examples of the activity of the imagination; a further illustration is afforded by artistic activity as well as by those symbolic devices for facilitating thought which are found even in science, where it is most strictly rational.

We do not readily perceive at a first glance why it is so comparatively often the case that adaptation can only be achieved in these regressive *détours*. Probably the true position is that in his ego, especially as expressed in rational thought and action, in its synthetic and differentiating function,[9] man is equipped with a very highly differenti-

---

[8] Cf. Anna Freud, *The Ego and the Mechanisms of Defence*, tr. by Cecil Baines (New York: International Universities Press, 1948).

[9] Cf. also Fuchs, "Zum Stand der heutigen Biologie," *Imago*, XXII (1936).

ated organ of adaptation but that this highly differentiated organ is evidently by itself incapable of guaranteeing an optimum of adaptation. A system of regulation operating at the highest level of development is not sufficient to maintain a stable equilibrium; a more primitive system is needed to supplement it.

The objections which we felt obliged to raise against the definitions of mental health and illness last mentioned (in connection with the problems of defense, regression, etc.) may be summarized as follows: these conceptions of health approach the problem too exclusively from the angle of the neuroses or rather they are formulated in terms of contrast with the neuroses. Mechanisms, developmental stages, modes of reaction, with which we have become familiar for the part they play in the development of the neuroses, are automatically relegated to the realm of the pathological —health is characterized as a condition in which these elements are absent. But the contrast thus established with the neuroses can have no meaning so long as we fail to appreciate how much of these mechanisms, developmental stages and modes of reaction is active in healthy individuals or in the development of those who later become so, i.e., so long as an analytical "normal psychology" is still very largely nonexistent. This is one of the reasons why it is precisely the analysis of conduct adapted to reality which is today considered of such importance.

I should add that the arbitrary nature of such definitions of mental health and illness is very much less evident in the literature of psychoanalysis itself than in many of its applications to social conditions, artistic activity, scientific production, etc. Where ethical, esthetic, and political valuations enter very clearly into play and proceed to make use of the concept of health for their special purposes, a considerably wider latitude is allowed to such arbitrary judgment. By skillful conjuring with these kinds of standards it becomes easy enough to prove that those who do not share our political or general outlook on life are neurotic or psychotic or that social conditions to which we are for some reason opposed are to be accounted as pathological. I believe that we are all clear in our own minds that such judgments—whether we personally share them or not—have no right to speak in the name of psychoanalytical science.

It will now have become quite obvious to us where many of the conceptions of health and illness discussed in this paper stand most in need of amplification, namely in the direction of the subject's relations with and adaptation to reality. I do not mean to suggest that in these attempts to formulate a definition, to arrive at a theoretical concept of health, the factor of adaptation has been neglected; this is very far from being the case. But in the form in which it is expressed the concept of adaptation itself is in many respects too ill-defined—and, as we have already remarked, "conduct adapted to reality" has hitherto offered little opportunity for a psychoanalytical approach.

It is obvious that what we designate as health or illness is intimately bound up with the individual's adaptation to reality (or, in the terms of an oft-repeated formula, with his sense of self-preservation). I have recently made an attempt to probe more deeply into the problems which confront psychoanalysis at this juncture.[10] Here I shall confine myself to a few suggestions which may seem worth considering in framing a definition of health. The individual's

[10] See "Ich-Psychologie und Anpassungsproblem," *Internationale Zeitschrift für Psychoanalyse und Imago*, XXIV (1939).

adjustment to reality may be opposed to that of the race. Now it is true that we are accustomed, from the standpoint of our therapeutic aims, to allow a substantial margin of priority to the claims of individual adaptation over those of the race. But if we are to insist that some connection exists between mental health and adaptation, we are bound to admit in the light of our previous remarks that the concept of health may bear inconsistent meanings according to whether we think of it in relation to the individual or to the community. Moreover, we shall deem it expedient to distinguish between the state of being adapted and the process by which it is achieved. And lastly we must point out that adaptation is only capable of definition in relation to something else, with reference to specific environmental settings. The actual state of equilibrium achieved in a given individual tells us nothing of his capacity for adaptation so long as we have not investigated his relations with the external world. Thus an unhampered "capacity for achievement and enjoyment," simply considered in isolation, has nothing decisive to tell us concerning the capacity for adapting oneself to reality. On the other hand disturbances in one's capacity for achievement and enjoyment (for the sake of simplicity we will keep to these familiar criteria) are not to be evaluated simply as a sign of failure in adaptation. This really goes without saying and I only mention it because it is occasionally overlooked when attempts are made to formulate a definition. As an indispensable factor in assessing an individual's powers of adaptation we would single out his relation to a "typical average environment." We must take account of all these aspects of the concept of adaptation if we are to establish criteria of health based on adaptation or the capacity for it. We would insist that the processes of adaptation are always appropriate only to a limited range of environmental conditions; and that successful efforts at adaptation toward specific external situations may in indirect ways lead at the same time to inhibitions in adaptation affecting the organism.

Freud[11] recently characterized this state of affairs by quoting Goethe's "Reason becomes unreason, beneficence a torment." Conversely, when viewed from this angle, the proposition that the nature of the environment may be such that a pathological development of the psyche offers a more satisfactory solution than would a normal one loses its paradoxical character.

This necessarily condensed presentation must inevitably make the considerations here adumbrated appear somewhat arid; but I am convinced that no analyst would have any difficulty in illustrating them from his clinical experience. In this connection I should like to insist once more that we shall obviously be in a better position to correlate all these definitions with concrete, clinically manifest conditions and thus to apply the concept of health in an unequivocal and trustworthy manner, when we have been able to advance further in the sphere of analytical "normal psychology," in the analysis of adapted behavior. I believe that a more attentive examination of the phenomena of adaptation may also help us to escape from the opposition between "biological" and "sociological" conceptions of mental development which plays a certain part in analysis but is fundamentally sterile. It is only when we consider the social phenomena of adaptation in their biological aspect that we can really start "getting psychology rightfully

[11] See "Analysis Terminable and Interminable," *International Journal of Psycho-Analysis*, XVIII (1937).

placed in the hierarchy of science, namely as one of the biological sciences."[12]

It is important that we should clearly realize both that there exists a close connection between adaptation and synthesis, and the extent of this. An "organization of the organism," the specific representative of which in the mental sphere we bring into relation with the synthetic function (and also with the differentiating function which has, however, been less fully explored), is a prerequisite of successful adaptation; on the other hand its efficacy is doubtless dependent on the measure of adaptation achieved. A process when viewed "from within" may often present itself as a disturbance of mental harmony; when viewed "from without" we should have to characterize the same process as a disturbance of adaptation. So, too, instinctual conflicts are very frequently bound up with a disturbed relation to the environment. It is also significant in this connection that the same process of defense quite commonly serves the twofold purpose of acquiring mastery over the instincts and of reaching an accommodation with the external world.

By thus seeking to make adaptation, and especially synthesis, the basis of our concept of health, we seem to have arrived at an "evolutionary" concept of health. And in point of fact this does represent a psychoanalytical contribution to the concept of mental health which should not be underestimated. But on the other hand a conception which relates the degree of mental health to the degree of development actually attained (compare the factor of rational control and, on the instinctual plane, the attainment of the genital stage as a prerequisite of health) suffers from

---

[12] Ernest Jones, "Psycho-Analysis and the Instincts," *Papers on Psycho-Analysis* (5th ed.; Baltimore: Williams and Wilkins, 1950).

certain limitations, at least as regards the ego, to which I have briefly alluded.

I shall here conclude this necessarily schematic and fragmentary presentation. I have endeavored to explain and discuss a number of standpoints which psychoanalysis has in fact adopted toward the concept of health, either expressly or by implication. In a one-sided fashion I proceeded to single out for almost exclusive attention those conditions of mental health which are seen to be related to the ego. I purposely restricted myself in this way. It seemed to me that there were good reasons why the psychology of the id had failed to provide us with a key to the problems of mental health. Moreover, by conducting my survey from the standpoint of the ego I found myself in a position to discuss certain problems of ego theory which are decidedly no less important than the question of our criteria of health. The contribution that I myself have been able to make toward the further development and criticism of these views certainly does not as yet enable us to formulate a concept of mental health in simple, unequivocal, definitive terms. But I believe that it will have helped us to discern quite clearly in which direction these prolegomena to a future analytical theory of health must be developed.

This article was originally published in the *International Journal of Psycho-Analysis*, Vol. XX, 1939.

Heinz Hartmann belongs to what we should now call the "second generation" of Freudian psychoanalysts. He became well-known for his development of the theory of ego psychology and he also served as a president of the International Psycho-Analytical Association.

Some biopsychical aspects of sado-masochism

Marie Bonaparte

We all know Freud's two theories of sado-masochism. The first, originally presented in *Three Essays on the Theory of Sexuality* (1905) reads thus:

> The most common and the most significant of all perversions—the desire to inflict pain upon the sexual object and its reverse—received from Krafft-Ebing the names of "sadism" and "masochism" for its active and passive forms respectively. Other writers have preferred the narrower term "algolagnia." This emphasizes the pleasure in *pain*, the cruelty; whereas the names chosen by Krafft-Ebing bring into prominence the pleasure in any form of humiliation or subjection.

> As regards active algolagnia, sadism, the roots are easy to detect in the normal. The sexuality of most male human beings contains an element of *aggressiveness*—and a desire to subjugate; the biological significance of it seems to lie in the need for overcoming the resistance of the sexual object by means other than the process of wooing. Thus sadism would correspond to an aggressive component of the sexual instinct which has become independent and exaggerated and, by displacement, has usurped the leading position.

> In ordinary speech the connotation of sadism oscillates between, on the one hand, cases merely characterized by an active or violent attitude to the sexual object, and, on the

other hand, cases in which satisfaction is entirely conditional on the humiliation and maltreatment of the object. Strictly speaking, it is only this last extreme instance which deserves to be described as a perversion.

Similarly, the term masochism comprises any passive attitude toward sexual life and the sexual object, the extreme instance of which appears to be that in which satisfaction is conditional upon suffering physical or mental pain at the hands of the sexual object. Masochism, in the form of a perversion, seems to be further removed from the normal sexual aim than its counterpart; it may be doubted at first sight whether it can ever occur as a primary phenomenon or whether, on the contrary, it may not invariably arise from a transformation of sadism. It can often be shown that masochism is nothing more than an extension of sadism turned round upon the subject's own self, which thus, to begin with, takes the place of the sexual object. Clinical analysis of extreme cases of masochistic perversion shows that a great number of factors (such as castration complex and the sense of guilt) have combined to exaggerate and fixate the original passive sexual attitude.

The history of human civilization shows beyond any doubt that there is an intimate connection between cruelty and the sexual instinct; but nothing has been done toward explaining the connection, apart from laying emphasis upon the aggressive factor in the libido. According to some authorities this aggressive element of the sexual instinct is in reality a relic of cannibalistic desires—that is, it is a contribution derived from the apparatus for obtaining mastery, which is concerned with the satisfaction of the other and, ontogenetically, the older of the great instinctual needs. It has also been maintained that every pain contains in itself the possibility of a feeling of pleasure. All that need be said is that no satisfactory explanation of this perversion has been put forward and that it seems possible that a number of mental impulses are combined in it to produce a single resultant.

But the most remarkable feature of this perversion is that its active and passive forms are habitually found to occur together in the same individual. A person who feels pleasure in producing pain in someone else during a sexual connection, is also capable of enjoying as pleasure any pain which he may himself derive from sexual relations. A sadist is always at the same time a masochist, although the active or the passive aspect of the perversion may be more strongly developed in him and may represent his predominant sexual activity.

We find, then, that certain among the impulses to perversion occur regularly as pairs of opposites; and this, taken in conjunction with material which will be brought forward later, has a high theoretical significance. It is, moreover, a suggestive fact that the existence of the pair of opposites formed by sadism and masochism cannot be attributed merely to the element of aggressiveness. We should rather be inclined to connect the simultaneous presence of these opposites with the opposing masculinity and femininity which are combined in bisexuality—a contrast which often has to be replaced in psychoanalysis by that between activity and passivity.

In a later work, *Instincts and their Vicissitudes* (1915), Freud, still maintaining his first theory of instincts, wrote:

. . . Whether there is, besides this, a more direct masochistic satisfaction is highly doubtful. A primary masochism not derived in the manner I have described from sadism, does not appear to be met with.

The conception of sadism is made more complicated by the circumstance that this instinct, side by side with its general aim (or perhaps rather, within it), seems to press toward a quite special aim: the infliction of pain, in addition to subjection and mastery of the object. Now psychoanalysis would seem to show that the infliction of pain plays no part in the original aims sought by the instinct: the sadistic child takes no notice of whether or not it inflicts pain, nor is it part of its purpose to do so. But when once the transformation into masochism has taken place, the experience of pain is very well adapted to serve as a passive masochistic aim, for we have every reason to believe that sensations of pain, like other unpleasant sensations, extend into sexual excitation and produce a condition which is pleasurable, for the sake of which the subject will even willingly experience the unpleasantness of pain. Where once the suffering of pain has been experienced as a masochistic aim, it can be carried back into the sadistic situation and result in a sadistic aim of *inflicting pain*, which will then be masochistically enjoyed by the subject while inflicting pain upon others, through this identification of himself with the suffering object. Of course, in either case it is not the pain itself which is enjoyed, but the accompanying sexual excitement, and this is especially easy for the sadist. The enjoyment of pain would thus be a primary masochistic aim, which, however, can then also become the aim of the originally sadistic instinct.

If we compare these two extracts we grasp the difficulty which Freud confronted in presenting his first concept of sado-masochism. Whatever he may first have thought, sadism could never be primary, for how could pleasure be felt in inflicting pain if one had not already experienced both these antagonistic and mysteriously linked sensations?

Passivity, generally, precedes activity. Freud thus comes to deny that any real primary sadism exists, since he denies the child any pleasure in its cruelty, widespread though that is, which hardly seems to conform to the facts.

With his second theory of instincts, however, Freud was to go much further along the path leading to the acceptance of masochism as the forerunner of true sadism, and even so far as to deny the existence of this primary phase of primitive infantile sadism which cannot yet be qualified as true sadism, and which is precisely our own point of view.

In *Beyond the Pleasure Principle* (1920), Freud abandons the dualism of ego and sexual instincts in his first theory of instincts, and establishes his second theory restoring this dualism to the death and life instincts, the latter taking to themselves the libidinal object drives and primary ego instincts which become the narcissistic libido.

As to the death instincts, there described for the first time, their tendency would be to return all living substance to its original inorganic condition. Nevertheless, the aggression which animates all creatures still remained unexplained, and it was not until *The Economic Problem of Masochism* (1924) was published that Freud's views on the subject became clear, and precisely on this subject of sado-masochism.

We have a right to describe the existence of the masochistic trend in the life of the human instincts as from the economic point of view mysterious. For if mental processes are governed by the pleasure principle, so that avoidance of "pain" and obtaining pleasure is their first aim, masochism is incomprehensible. If physical pain and feelings of distress can cease to be signals of danger and be ends in themselves, the pleasure principle is paralyzed, the watchman of our mental life is to all intents and purposes himself drugged and asleep.

In this light, masochism appears to us as a great danger, which is in no way true of sadism, its counterpart. We feel tempted to call the pleasure principle the watchman of our lives, instead of only the watchman of our mental life. But then the question of the relation of the pleasure principle to the two varieties of instincts that we have distinguished, the *death instincts* and the *erotic (libidinal) life instincts* demands investigation . . .*

---

* *Author's italics.*

Freud then posits three types of masochism; erotogenic, feminine, and moral, and, after describing the feminine masochism observed by him in various male patients who delighted in being, or imagining themselves, "pinioned, bound, beaten painfully, whipped, in some way mishandled, forced to obey unconditionally, defiled, degraded," he concludes that "the feminine type of masochism . . . is based entirely on the primary erotogenic type, on the 'lust of pain' which cannot be explained without going very far back."

Now follows the backward glance which Freud invites us to take:

In my *Drei Abhandlungen zur Sexual-theorie*, in the section on the sources of infantile sexuality, I put forward the proposition that sexual excitation arises as an accessory effect of a large series of internal processes *as soon as the intensity of these pleasures has exceeded certain quantitative limits*,* indeed, that perhaps nothing very important takes place within the organism without contributing a component to the excitation of the sexual instinct. According to this, an excitation of physical pain and feelings of distress would surely also have this effect. This *libidinal sympathetic excitation** accompanying the tension of physical pain and feelings of distress would be an infantile physiological mechanism which ceases to operate later on. It would reach a varying degree of development in different sexual constitutions; in any case it would provide the physiological foundation on which the structure of erotogenic masochism is subsequently erected in the mind.

The inadequacy of this explanation is seen, however, in that it throws no light on the regular and close connection of masochism with *sadism*,* its counterpart in the life of the instincts. If we go a step further back to our hypothesis of

---

* *Author's italics.*

the two varieties of instincts which we believe to be active in animate beings, we come to another conclusion which, however, does not contradict the one just mentioned. In the multicellular living organism the libido meets the death or destruction instinct which holds sway there, and which tries to disintegrate this cellular being and bring each elemental primary organism into a condition of inorganic stability (though this again may be but relative). To the libido falls the task of making this destructive instinct harmless, and it manages to dispose of it by directing it to a great extent and early in life—with the help of a special organic system, the musculature—toward the objects of the outer world. It is then called the instinct of destruction, of mastery, the will to power. A section of this instinct is placed directly in the service of the sexual function, where it has an important part to play: this is true *sadism*.* Another part is not included in this displacement outwards; it remains within the organism and is "bound" there libidinally with the help of the accompanying sexual excitation mentioned above: this we must recognize as the original *erotogenic masochism*.*

We are entirely without any understanding of the physiological ways and means by which this subjugation of the death instinct by the libido can be achieved. In the psychoanalytical world of ideas we can only assume that a very extensive coalescence and fusion, varying according to conditions, of the two instincts takes place, so that we never have to deal with pure life instincts and death instincts at all, but only with combinations of them in different degrees. Corresponding with the fusion of instincts there may under certain influences occur a "defusion" of them. How large a part of the death instincts may refuse to be subjugated in this way by becoming attached to libidinal quantities it is at present not possible to ascertain.

If one is willing to disregard a certain amount of inexacti-

---

* *Author's italics.*

tude, it might be said that the death instinct active in the organism—the primal sadism—is identical with masochism. After the chief part of it has been directed outwards toward objects, there remains as a residuum within the organism the true erotogenic masochism, which on the one hand becomes a component of the libido and on the other still has the subject itself for an object. So that this masochism would be a witness and a survival of that phase of development in which the amalgamation, so important for life afterwards, of death instinct and Eros took place. We should not be astonished to hear that under certain conditions the sadism or destruction instinct which has been directed outwards can be introjected, turned inward again, regressing in this way to its earlier condition. It then provides that *secondary masochism** which supplements the original one.

The erotogenic type of masochism passes through all the developmental stages of the libido, and from them it takes the changing shapes it wears in the life of the mind. The fear of being devoured by the totem animal (father) is derived from the primitive oral stage of libido organization; the desire to be beaten by the father from the next following sadistic-anal stage; castration, although it is subsequently denied, enters into the content of masochistic fantasies as a residue from the phallic stage; and from the final genital stage are derived of course the situations characteristic of womanhood, namely, the passive part in coitus and the act of giving birth. The part played by the nates in masochism is also easily intelligible, apart from its obvious foundation in reality. The nates are the special erotogenic bodily regions which have preference in the sadistic-anal stage, as the nipple in the oral stage and the penis in the genital stage.

Freud then goes at length into the question of moral masochism, which plays so great a part in so many lives as the need for punishment and the tendency to frustration.

---

* *Author's italics.*

Highly desexualized though it may seem, this form of masochism also arises on the biological foundation of erotogenic masochism. We shall not, however, continue to follow Freud here, since our main inquiry is into the biopsychical origins of erotogenic sado-masochism.

But first another voice merits attention; that of the man from whom sadism takes its name.

In that verbose romance, *Histoire de Juliette: Les Prospérités du Vice*, the notorious Marquis de Sade intersperses his countless scenes of exquisite and cruel lust with metaphysical or philosophical discussions. I shall quote from among those where he seeks to justify what today we term sado-masochism.

Some noblemen, voluptuaries, admiringly described as "ferocious," have gathered, one evening, round a festive board which is lit by candles so stuck as to roast the private parts of a number of little girls. Our noblemen, however, complacently continue their philosophizing.

"Noirceuil," said Saint-Fond, "while our little novices roast, explain, I beg, with your usual metaphysics, how one may manage to obtain pleasure from watching the sufferings of others or from suffering oneself?" "Listen then," said Noirceuil, "and I will prove it to you."

"*Pain*, logically speaking, *is nothing but a feeling of aversion inspired in the soul by certain responses, opposed to its structure, in the body it animates.* So says Nicole, who distinguished an aerial substance in man which he termed soul, as opposed to the material substance we call body. Personally, since I do not at all accept that frivolous idea and see man only as a kind of purely concrete vegetation, I would merely say that pain is a consequence of the disharmony between foreign bodies and the organic molecules of which we are constituted, with the result that the atoms emanated by these foreign bodies, instead of attaching themselves to our nervous fluid, as they do in the shock of pleasure, only make an angular, prickly, repellent approach, so that they never link up together. Yet, though their effects are repellent they are nevertheless always effects and, whether it be pleasure or pain we are offered, they will always provoke a shock to the nervous fluid. Now, what is to prevent this shock of pain, infinitely keener and more vigorous than the other, from exciting in this fluid that same widespread conflagration which arises through attachment of the atoms emanated by objects of pleasure? If we must have sensations, what is to prevent one getting used, through habit, to being made just as happy through the repellent atoms as through those which attach? Satiated with the effects of those which produce only simple sensations, why should I not get equally used to receiving pleasure from those which give *poignant* sensations? They both strike in the same place, the only difference being that while one is keen, the other is mild and, to be satiated, is not the former infinitely preferable to the latter? Do we not, every day, see folk who have accustomed their palates to an irritation they like, and others who could not endure that irritation for a moment? And is it not nowadays true (once you grant my hypothesis) that, in their pleasures, men always try to rouse the objects that serve their enjoyment in the same way that they themselves are roused, and that this practice, in the metaphysics of enjoyment, is considered as resulting from 'delicacy'? What is there strange, then, in a man, endowed with the organs we describe, by the same practices as his adversary and acting on the same principles of delicacy, imagining he will stir the object that serves his enjoyment by means that affect him himself? He has done no worse than the other, he has only done what the other did. The consequences differ, I agree, but the original motives are the same: the former was no crueler than the latter, and neither of the two has done wrong; both, on the object of their enjoyment, have used the identical means they employ to get pleasure.

"But, the creature at the mercy of a brutal lust will reply: *That does not please me*; in which case I must see whether I can compel you to like it or not. If I cannot, go away and let me be; if, on the other hand, my money, credit or position give me some mastery over you or some earnest that I can abolish your objections, then silently suffer whatever I may please to impose, because enjoyment I must have, and I can only enjoy by tormenting you and seeing your tears flow. In any case, do not be surprised, or blame me at all, because I obey the motions with which nature endowed me, or follow the path she makes me take; in a word, by subjecting you to my harsh and brutal lusts, those alone which succeed in bringing me to the acme of pleasure, I act from those same principles of delicacy as the effeminate lover who only knows the roses of a feeling which I can but see as thorns. For, in tormenting and rending you, I do the only thing by which I am stirred, just as he, drearily raking his mistress, does the only thing that stirs him agreeably. Let us leave effeminate delicacy to him, however, because it could never stir such powerfully made organs as mine. Yes, friends," continued Noirceuil, "you may be sure that no being, truly passionate for the joys of lust, could ever indeed mix delicacy with it, that delicacy which merely poisons these pleasures and implies a sharing that is impossible to whoever seeks real pleasure: any power shared is weakened thereby. It is a commonplace that, if you try to give enjoyment to the object that serves your pleasure, you will soon see it is at your own expense. There is no passion more egotistic than that of sensuality; not one that demands to be served more sternly. One must absolutely never think about anyone but oneself, when in erection, and never consider the object that serves us except as a kind of victim offered to the rage of that passion. Do not all passions demand victims? Well, the passive object, in the lust act, is that of our lustful rage; the less it is spared, the better the aim is fulfilled; the keener that object's pangs, the more utterly is it degraded and humbled and the more complete is our enjoyment. It is not pleasure we should make that object taste, but sensations that we should produce in it and, since that of pain is infinitely keener than that of pleasure, it is indubitable that it is better for the shock this outer sight produces on our nerves to happen through pain, rather than pleasure. There you have the explanation of the mania of those numerous libertines who, like ourselves, never manage to achieve erections and seminal emissions except by committing acts of atrocious cruelty, or by gorging themselves on their victim's blood.[1] Some would not even experience the slightest erection, despite the worst extremities of pain in their object, but for the thought that they themselves were the prime cause of those pangs in the sorry thing sold to their lustful rage. You desire to subject your nerves to a violent shock, you feel that that of pain will be stronger than that of pleasure, you use those means and find yourself well contented. But beauty, some idiot objects, softens and moves; it urges to kindness, pardon. How resist a pretty girl's tears when, with clasped hands, she implores her torturer? Well, indeed! that's just what one wants; it is the very prerequisite from which the libertine in question derives all his delightful enjoyment; he would indeed deserve to be pitied were he acting on an inert, unfeeling creature, and this objection is as ridiculous as would be a man's who declared one should never eat mutton because the sheep is an inoffensive creature."

Comparing these extracts with Freud's hypothesis of the origins of sado-masochism, we see that de Sade, evidently at first hand, seems to subscribe in advance to the first Freudian concept of masochism, forerunner of true sadism, as expressed in *Instincts and their Vicissitudes*.

---

[1] As did Kürten, the vampire of Düsseldorf.

Where once the suffering of pain has been experienced as a masochistic aim, it can be carried back into the sadistic situation and result in a sadistic aim of *inflicting pain*, which will then be masochistically enjoyed by the subject while inflicting pain upon others, through his identification of himself with the suffering object.

In other pages, however, and best in the words he lends Pope Braschi, de Sade even seems to go so far as to accept the Freudian concept of the death instincts, every whit as eternal and dominant as the life instincts, as in this dithyramb by his mitred philosopher.

"In all beings, the principle of life is no other than that of death: we receive and foster them in us, both at the same time. In that instant we call *death*, everything seems to disintegrate: we believe so, owing to the extreme change then found in this portion of matter which no longer seems animate. This death, however, is but imaginary; it is merely figurative and without reality. Matter, bereft of that subtle portion of matter which communicated motion to it, is not thereby destroyed; it merely changes its form, it corrupts, and already you see a proof of the activity it retains in it; it gives sap to the earth, fertilizes it, and serves to regenerate other kingdoms, besides its own. In fine, there is no essential difference between the first life we receive and this second which is that we call death. For the first comes about through the matter formed and organized in the female womb and the second, likewise, from the matter renewed and reorganized in the bowels of the earth. Thus, in its new womb, this extinguished matter again becomes the germ of particles of etherealized matter which, but for it, would have remained apparently inert. There you have all the wisdom of the laws governing these three kingdoms, laws they received on their first irruptions, laws which confine nature's urges to gush forth in new ways; these are the only ways in which the laws inherent to these kingdoms operate. The first generation, which we call life, provides us with a sort of example. These laws only succeed in reaching the first generation through exhaustion; they do not reach the other save by destruction. For the former a sort of corrupt matter is needed; for the second, putrified matter. That is the sole cause of these huge successive creations; in one and all there are but these prime principles of exhaustion or annihilation, which thus makes clear that death is as necessary as life, that there is no death and that all the scourges we have mentioned . . . (those wars and famines with which she (nature) overwhelms us, those pestilences which, from time to time, she visits on the globe in order to destroy us, those scoundrels she multiplies, those Alexanders, Tamerlanes, Genghis Khans, all those heroes who ravage the earth) . . . the tyrants' cruelty, the villain's crimes, are as necessary to the laws of these three kingdoms as are the deeds which rebrought them to life; that, when nature visits them on the earth, meaning to annihilate these kingdoms which deprive it of the capacity to produce new upsurges, it merely performs an impotent act, since the first laws received by these kingdoms when they first gushed forth, stamped this productive capacity upon them for ever and ever; this, nature could never abolish except by totally destroying herself, which is not in her power, since she herself is subject to laws from whose sway it is impossible for her to escape, and which will endure eternally. Thus the villain, by his murders, not only assists nature's intentions towards ends she will never be able to fulfill, but even assists the laws which the kingdoms received at their first upsurge. I say first upsurge, to ease comprehension of my system, for since there never was an act of creation and since nature is eternal, the gushes are perpetual while creatures exist; they would cease to be, if no more occurred, and would then encourage secondary gushes, which are those that nature desires but to which she cannot attain except by total destruction, the intended aim of crime. Whence it results that the criminal who could overwhelm all three kingdoms at once by annihilating them and their productive capacities would be he who had served nature best.

Thus, the anthropomorphized sadism of nature, which Goethe personified in Mephisto as "the spirit that always denies," would prevail, and the ultimate trend of the death instincts postulated by Freud would have overshot their mark: that of the return of organic matter to the inorganic state.

I do not, of course, imagine that the death instincts, as conceived by de Sade, are identical with those philosophically postulated by Freud. I merely wish to draw attention to some rough, though interesting, points of agreement.

Nevertheless, despite de Sade, and even Freud, the cardinal problem of sado-masochism in which Pleasure and Pain, Libido and Destruction, are so enigmatically, so paradoxically intertwined, does not seem entirely solved.

I say Destruction and not Death, for, to me, the destructive and aggressive instincts are not identical in essence, as regards that silent fading into the inorganic of all things living as they move toward death. This seems to me, as to other analysts, an entropy as it were, a running down of the life force, which must be "unlived," faster or slower, in each species, through life. Does not Freud himself allude to this, in *Beyond the Pleasure Principle*, in regard to the transient rejuvenation of living substance by conjugation of the reproductive cells?

Nor is it very clear how a simple entropy, a negative concept such as the dissipation of energy, can turn outwards and assume the active, positive form of living aggression. Aggression seems much more wholly to derive from life and its cravings. In any case, aggression is not a hypothesis but an observable fact.

And the just as obvious fact of sado-masochism, in which, whether active or passive, Destruction mingles inextricably with Libido, continues to challenge all our sagacity.

Where greater men than ourselves have tried, dare we venture to cast some light into such darkness?

It is clinically in the pervert that masochism as an entity is met. It has already been described; the need to be bound, beaten, humiliated, or suffer in different ways in order to achieve sexual enjoyment.

It is clinically, too, in the sadist, that sadism is met, with its manifold cruelty and the frightful lust murders committed by these rare criminal perverts who, from time to time, terrify yet enthrall the public.

What roots are we to postulate for such extremes of sadism, as of masochism? There seem to be several, some biological, others psychological.

The living cell is a speck of protoplasm bounded by a more or less protective membrane. The cell is not, however, hermetically sealed; it not only receives impressions, but can be entered in three ways.

For nutrition, it must draw such substances from its environment as are needed to keep it alive; to assimilate and reject.

For reproduction, if a female cell, it must undergo penetration by another living cell; be impregnated by the male cell. Both these penetrations are beneficent and serve life. They differ from each other in that the nutritive process works on organic though dead substances, substances which have lost their living identity and can only at that price become part of the cell that ingests them, whereas impregnation is unique in that one live cell is penetrated by another and does not undergo destruction and death but, on the contrary, creates life.

The third sort of cellular penetration is traumatic: infraction and wounding causing suffering and death.

If we now apply all this to multicellular organisms, we also find these three possible kinds of penetration which, as regards the penetrated organism, imply three different kinds of response:

Appetite for substances able to serve nutrition;

Erotic attraction toward the sexual partner;

Terror of infraction and wounding that may cause suffering and death.

In the animal world, however, at a certain point in the scale, internal fecundation is established. Not only the sex cell, the ovum, must be penetrated, but the very body of the female, by the penis. It is so with all mammals.

As a result a psychical confusion may arise in the female between the erotic and the wounding penetration, whence results the flight from the male of many mammalian females and, in our own species, so many cases of feminine frigidity.

Erotism, however, tends to bind this terror of infraction and often succeeds, either by largely masochizing the confusion between wounding and erotogenic penetration, or by establishing such penetration as preeminently erotogenic. Nevertheless, some homeopathic dose of masochism remains needful for acceptance of even the most erotogenic feminine penetration.

Even to Krafft-Ebing, years ago, masochism seemed, in fact, "a sort of pathological overgrowth of psychical feminine factors; a sort of morbid intensification of certain psychic characteristics of women."

Freud too, as we saw in his *Three Essays*, wrote that "we should rather be inclined to connect the simultaneous presence of these opposites" (sado-masochism) "with the opposing masculinity and femininity which are combined in bisexuality—a contrast which often has to be replaced in psychoanalysis by that between activity and passivity."

I do not know whether some unimaginable, basic masochism exists in the cell, or what forms masochism may assume in the course of evolution, but, to me, it seems that the erotogenic masochism of the totality of a multicellular organism could only truly appear when internal fecundation had been established.

Thereupon the same confusion between erotogenic and wounding penetration which, so often, makes the mammalian female flee from the male, may operate in the contrary manner. We then find ourselves faced, in that crown of nature which is man, by those final forms of erotogenic masochism whose clinical shapes we know. Only the vital biological instinct of self-preservation can then halt the erotically wished for aggression at the point where danger to life would begin.

These, then, would be the phylogenetic roots of human masochism which plunge into man's remotest evolutionary past. Thus, through countless ages, erotism would be linked with every infraction, every disturbance of living tissue, including unpleasure and pain.

We may also, however, seek the biological roots of masochism ontogenetically.

When does the human child apprehend, following the laws which govern its species, that it is destined to perpetuate itself through internal impregnation? Something, in the depths of its tissue, may well sense it. Yet, from this angle, a primordial happening in childhood must instruct it as to its future destiny as man or woman; that primal scene which so many children have witnessed, while the adults imagine them too young to notice. Observation of the coupling of animals, in any case, is never absent from an infantile anamnesis and provides a substitute from which the child will imagine what happens between the parents.

Psychoanalytic observation enables us to establish that coitus is always interpreted, by the childish observer, as a brutal, aggressive act, committed by the male on the female; that is the sadistic concept of coitus. Then, depending upon the amount of masculinity or femininity it includes, the child will thenceforth identify itself predominantly with either the man or the woman, but, always, given its original bisexuality, in some degree with both.

If the child is a girl, fear of male aggression may result, depending on the degree of masculinity she harbors, and lead to a re-cathecting of her defensive masculine positions. Unless, that is, a truly feminine masochism is constituted. If the child, however, is male, his masochism, also, may become strengthened, depending on the degree of innate femininity present, though sadism should predominate in some acceptable form. As though the little male already felt that penetration would be spared him; that, like the spermatozoon which would later shoot from his body, he too, luckier than the female, would not be penetrated but penetrate.

Thus, from the memory of the primal scene, lost in the mists of infantile amnesis, and from the traces which it leaves in each unconscious, the resulting sadistic concept of coitus may make the female draw back from accepting the penetrative phallus, imaginarily likened to some piercing weapon. But it may also, at times, in the sadistically predisposed male, create the very counterpart to this sadistic concept of coitus in which the erotogenic concept of wounding, of a piercing weapon, is phallicized and eroticized. In that case the phallic symbolism of the knife is taken literally by the mind.

It is this erotogenic concept of the wound that the great sadists like Kürten or Vacher expressed concretely, and that Baudelaire sang, in such sublimated form, in his poem "A celle qui est trop gaie."[2] No more poetic or clearer expression could be given to this confusion between penetration in its wounding and erotic aspects. It is not only the phallic symbolism of the knife that shows through here, but the poison symbolism of semen which so many neurotic symptoms reveal. So classical, so transparent, are the sadistic symbols of the poem, that the judges immediately sensed them when this poem in *Les Fleurs du Mal* was condemned as obscene. Yet these are universal sexual symbols which only the unique span of the human imagination could contrive. We must now turn to its other achievements.

There are forces other than biological, however, which help to make human beings masochistic or sadistic; psychological forces which bring into play the psychical mechanisms of associated ideas and imaginative identification with others.

---

[2] Mad woman who maddens me,
I hate thee as much as I love thee!

Thus, I would like, some night,
When the hour of lust strikes,
To crawl, I, a craven, in silence,
Towards the treasures that are thine.

In order to chastise thy joyous flesh,
To bruise thy pardoned breast
And to inflict on thy surprised flank
A deep and hollow wound.

And, giddy with the sweetness of it,
Through these new lips of thine
More beautiful and more radiant,
Infuse in thee my venom, O sister of mine!

—*Translated by Marie Bonaparte*

The universe is full of hostile forces which deny the child and individual the satisfaction which their instincts desire. From birth, from the cradle, it is at the mercy of hunger and cold, for the mother or breast do not always turn up in time to soothe it when needed. Later, privations, accidents, punishments cannot always be avoided. Nevertheless, the pleasure principle reigns deep in the young creature and tends to over-cathect even painful emotions and feelings as, for instance, the whippings of ill-inspired upbringers. Doubtless that is why, as Freud says: "It may well be that nothing of considerable importance can occur in the organism without contributing some component to the excitation of the sexual instinct"[3] which would therefore, *par excellence*, be the hedonistic instinct. Thus "an excitation of physical pain and feelings of distress would surely also have this effect."[4]

The mechanism governing the association of ideas being thus actuated, with pleasure arising at the same time as pain, certain kinds of pain soon seem to be sought for themselves, thus often establishing paradoxical hedonistic responses for life.

Since all beings are basically bisexual, however, every masochist is more or less a sadist, the male factor which he includes taking to itself the pleasure pain in order to project them centrifugally outwards in accordance with the objectives of convex masculine eroticism. Many women, also, may be sadistic, owing to the male element they include, but it is mainly among males that sadism assumes its most striking forms. Since the male, like the spermatozoon, is

---

[3] See *Three Contributions to the Theory of Sex*, tr. by A. A. Brill (New York: E. P. Dutton, 1963).

[4] See "The Economic Problem of Masochism," *Collected Papers*, (New York: Basic Books, 1959), II, 255.

not penetrated but penetrates another organism in the generative act, sadism is essentially male, as well as being vitally important.

Thus, when the pain pleasure pair have taken a centrifugal path and turned outwards, the vital instinct of self-preservation ceases to be threatened and no longer raises barriers against it. On the contrary, it combines with the sadism, which then, in possessive, destructive fashion strives to annex the maximum amount of living space round it, and to master and rule in supremely egotistic fashion. And the sadist will allow himself orgies of blood that the masochist must deny. Here enters the second and prime psychological condition needful to sadism, namely, human imagination, which allows that identification of aggressor with aggressed from which arise those intense, safe, and boundless masochistic pleasures, because imagined, which, when combined with the egocentric intoxication of power, find satisfaction in the cruelest lust.

Thus the sadist, in the integrity of his ego, in the security of his own body, delights in the pain he inflicts, as it were by proxy, much in the way we safely enjoy the dramatic mishaps of our tragedy heroes. But, a more powerful relish, the play is real and the triumph his own.

Again, the essential ambivalence of Eros finds satisfaction in sadism. Born of the lover's eternal but unattainable desire to unite with his beloved, this ambivalence craves the destruction of that object in order that the vain, and thus painful, striving may end. Yet, though the great criminal sadist will at times partially devour his victim, true union with her is still withheld, as to all lovers. Then only the destruction of that ephemeral plaything of his passion will establish a more or less enduring truce which, for a time, assuages the sadist's torturing, unappeasable desires.

Such seem to be some of the biological and psychological roots which help to give rise to the great masochists and sadists.

Fortunately, however, masochistic like sadistic drives do not culminate in such extremes of perseveration. And though we all retain some masochistic or sadistic infantile residues in the unconscious, it is mostly in *inhibited* or *transformed* shapes.

What inhibits masochism, as we have shown, is the limitation placed upon it by the vital instinct of self-preservation. What inhibits sadism is precisely that on which, in other cases, it rests; the psychical mechanism of identification.

Depending on whether the sadist, innately, is more or less masochistic, i.e., ready to cathect the experienced pain with pleasure, he will likewise enjoy inflicted pain by imaginatively placing himself in the position of the victim and will, in some degree, be sadistic. But if the barrier of the vital instinct of self-preservation in himself strongly opposes the masochism in him, the same barrier will function in the potential sadist against the infliction of pain on others, through identification with them. This mechanism which inhibits sadism through *reaction formation* we call pity. That is to say that the less innately masochistic one is, the less sadistic one will be, which is hardly surprising.

Sado-masochism may also be liable to vicissitudes other than those of *perseveration* or *inhibition* through *reaction formation*. It may also undergo a transformation destined to great achievements, that of *moralization*.

Human morality could never have arisen, through the ages, save by the strong repressing the weak, to which the weak, resentfully, submitted. Nevertheless, to endure this constraint they had, perforce, to eroticize such painful moral and, at times, physical pressure. This is still true today, even in enlightened homes. Analysis, however, has enabled us to see that the prohibitions instituted by the child's upbringers are introjected by degrees and, combined with the individual's internalized aggression, later constitute its superego or moral conscience. The masochism in the ego then maintains the child's masochistic attitude to the superego which, modeled on those who brought it up, will be harsh and even sadistic. By this employment of our universal sado-masochism, man's moral conscience has arisen.

In this *moralization* of sado-masochism, are we encountering a *sublimation* of these awe-inspiring drives? It may be so, since sublimation implies deflecting a drive to another than its original objective. Yet virtue is often so ferocious, both to oneself and others, that we may doubt whether such mobilization of sado-masochism can be called a true sublimation. All the more in that we find precisely these same self-torturing mechanisms at work at the roots of the psychoneuroses, which clearly reveals the basic ferocity of sado-masochism, even when transformed into moralistic shapes.

Moral masochism, though least spectacular, is the most widespread of all. To it many unfortunates owe their failure in life, and the more readily in that the blows they account to fate are often inflicted by those petty moral sadists who, like themselves, swarm everywhere. These petty moral sadists may be frankly malevolent or virtuous people, since virtue is often sadistic. In any case, moral masochists seem to invite the blows of their sadistically moral counterparts, which thus helps to turn their lives into an ever-thorny path.

Of the three noble entities praised by the Philosophers:

the Good, the Beautiful, the True: goodness, therefore, does not seem properly able to sublimate sado-masochism successfully.

Do the Beautiful and the True succeed any better?

It would seem so, for sadism feeds both the inquiring and the scientific spirit, though it is that sublimated sadism which, through the intellect, strives to penetrate the universal body. Only the surgeon reveals a certain regression, in this spirit, as actual penetrator of human flesh, though with permitted and beneficent intents.

The maximum sublimation of sado-masochism, however, is achieved by art; and that in its most direct though least concrete form, thanks to the incomparable power of human imagination. The great works of art are cruel, whether one thinks of Shakespeare's or Sophocles' tragedies, to mention but these. Nowadays the cinema, that mass substitute for antique tragedy, delights in murderous plots.

This salutary catharsis of the most dangerous human instincts may be experienced by the spectator without peril, as without remorse, for, peacefully seated in his place, he well knows that after the bloodiest death, the screen or play hero will have gone home to bed.

As for the creative artist, his achievements, issuing from instinctual depths, have no doubt often saved him from sadistic deeds by allowing him to act his sadism. What would a Poe or a Baudelaire have become, but for the safety valve of their sovereign art? Even a de Sade who, as a rarely gifted writer, could imaginatively indulge his monstrous sadism, was doubtless thus saved from committing worse crimes than savagely flogging a Rose Keller, or distributing sweets containing cantharides at an orgy.

Yet, from the example of the "divine Marquis," we can see how much more intensely sadism, i.e., imaginative masochism combined with a triumphant masculine egocentricity, fascinates man than its humble brother, primary masochism. For though the works of a Sacher-Masoch still keep their documentary value for the psychiatrist or psychologist, they cannot claim the enduring luster of the work of a de Sade. And that, even ignoring their unequal talents. The content here lends luster to the form, since sadism, compared with simple masochism, triumphs by linking the vital and male with the pleasure of inflicting pain.

Thus sado-masochism, whose roots plunge into the matrix of the first living tissue, penetrated now by life and again by death, beholds its rule confirmed in that internally impregnated mammal, man, due to the original confusion communicated to the total human body through the long chain of evolution. This is the biological, the phylogenetic determinant of sado-masochism.

This awareness that internal impregnation takes place finds additional confirmation in each generation by what the child experiences in witnessing the primal scene; from this arises the sadistic concept of coitus. In this concept the child, depending on the degree to which it is innately female or male, identifies itself more or less with the female or male adult. The foundations thereupon begin to be laid for a more or less sadistic or masochistic nature which will manifest itself later; this is the biological and ontogenetic determinant of sado-masochism.

The following determinants are more specifically psychological. Masochism, under the primacy of the pleasure principle and the inevitable suffering which life brings all creatures, becomes intensified by erotization, throughout childhood, which associated ideas should lead us to meet misfortune bravely.

If the child, however, declares itself more male than

female, its original sadism will dominate; this will serve to project the masochism outward through identification of aggressor with aggressed and thus enable the child to enjoy its masochistic pleasures in security, since they are mirror images, while remaining a conqueror itself. This triumph it owes to the illimitable imagination of man. In that respect the animal creation can never equal man, Taine's "fierce, lustful gorilla!" And the essential ambivalence of Eros, which blossoms in our species, finds gratification in the destruction of the sexual partner.

In that super-cerebral creature man, however, many different vicissitudes await his sado-masochism. His extreme *perseverations* which culminate in the great perversions are, happily, not the rule. As for the masochism, that is shackled by *inhibitions* and the vital instinct of self-preservation, whereas his sadism is inhibited by *pity*, which is also determined by identification, though no longer masochistic, with the possible victim. Another vicissitude to which sado-masochism is subject is that of *moralization*, accompanied by moral torturings of oneself and others. Finally, *sublimation*, its transmutation into Science and Art, is the most highly developed form which man can give to sado-masochism, for he then employs it to serve civilization.

Even in the highest cultures, however, human sado-masochism remains active, demanding and insatiate. The occasional perverts which it here and there produces; the spectacular recital of crimes in the press; the occasional executions that thrill the public; the moral masochism to which, more or less, every civilized being is subjected and the sublimations of science and art; often do not suffice man any longer. It is as though, in a nostalgia for its origins, it once more desired the penetration of flesh. So the sportsman kills for pleasure and the soldier for the fatherland or an ideal. Truly, though with grim irony, it has been said that the art of war is to convey as much metal as possible into the most human flesh, not to mention the vast ancillary destruction. True, aggression here seems stripped of eroticism. And yet, some echo of our primitive sado-masochistic reactions stirs deep in the hearts of the fighters, as of those in the rear who read, or hear, victorious communiqués announcing that twenty thousand tons of bombs, more or less, have been dropped on troop concentrations or populous towns.

It seems, indeed, that physical aggression, stripped of hedonistic appeal, that is, of all sadism, is impossible to that animal with imagination, man. And the vast blood bath of war enables sado-masochism to rediscover its original path on an immensely magnified scale, desexualized though it appear; that of the triumphant, death dealing penetration of the living body.

Herein lies an obstacle to any true conversion of the peoples' hearts to pacifism, despite the increasing horror of modern wars.

BIBLIOGRAPHY

Alexander, Franz. "The Need for Punishment and the Death-Instinct," *International Journal of Psycho-Analysis*, X, 1929.
Berg, Karl. "Der Sadist," *Deutsch Z.f.d. ges. gerichtiliche Med.*, XVII, 1931.
Bonaparte, Marie. "Passivity, Masochism and Femininity," *International Journal of Psycho-Analysis*, XVI, 1935.
———. "Some Palaeobiological and Biopsychical Reflections," *International Journal of Psycho-Analysis*, XIX, 1938.
———. "De la Sexualité de la Femme," *Revue Française de Psychanalyse*, XIII, 1949.
Deutsch, Helene. "The Significance of Masochism in the Mental Life of Women," *International Journal of Psycho-Analysis*, XI, 1930.
Ellis, Havelock. "Studies in the Psychology of Sex," *Society of Psychological Research*, 1904.

Federn, Paul. "Beiträge zur Analyse des Sadismus und Masochismus," *Internationale Zeitschrift für Psychoanalyse*, I and II, 1913–1914.

Freud, Sigmund. *Three Contributions to the Theory of Sex*. Tr. by A. A. Brill. New York: E. P. Dutton, 1963.

———. "Instincts and their Vicissitudes," tr. by Joan Rivière. *Collected Papers*, IV. New York: Basic Books, 1959.

———. "A Child is being Beaten," tr. by Joan Rivière. *Collected Papers*, II. New York: Basic Books, 1959.

———. *Beyond the Pleasure Principle*. Tr. by James Strachey. New York: W. W. Norton, 1961.

———. "The Economic Problem of Masochism," tr. by Joan Rivière. *Collected Papers*, II. New York: Basic Books, 1959.

Horney, Karen. "The Problem of Feminine Masochism," *Psychoanalytic Review*, 1935, XXII, 245–257.

Krafft-Ebing, Richard. *Psychopathia Sexualis*. New York: Putnam, 1965.

LaForgue, René. "De l'Angoisse à l'Orgasme," *Revue Française de Psychanalyse*, IV, 1930–31.

Meisenheimer, Johannes. *Geschlecht und Geschlechter*. (Jena, 1921.)

Nacht, S. and Loewenstein, R. "Le Masochisme," *Revue Française de Psychanalyse*, X, 1938.

Reich, Wilhelm. "Der Masochistische Charakter," *Internationale Zeitschrift für Psychoanalyse*, XVIII, 1932.

Reik, Theodor. *Geständniszwang und Strafbednürfnis*. (Wien, 1925.)

Sacher-Masoch, Leopold von. *Die Damen im Pelz*. 1881.

Sade, Donatien Alphonse François, Marquis de. *Justine: les Malheurs de la Vertu*. 1791.

———. *Histoire de Juliette: les Prospérités du Vice*. 1792.

———. *Les 120 Journées de Sodome*. 1800.

Sadger, Isidor. "Ein Beitrag zum Verständnis des Sado-Masochismus," *Internationale Zeitschrift für Psychoanalyse*, XII, 1926.

Weiss, Edoardo. "Todestrieb und Masochismus," *Internationale Zeitschrift für Psychoanalyse*, XXI, 1935.

This paper was read before the Seventeenth International Psycho-Analytical Congress in Amsterdam in 1951, and later appeared, in a translation by John Rodker, in the *International Journal of Psycho-Analysis,* Vol. XXXIII, 1952.

Marie Bonaparte was one of Freud's most cherished students. She became very close to him in his later years, and was active in the formation of the French Psychoanalytical Society. She has written extensively in the field of psychoanalysis and literature.

The problem of freedom in psychoanalysis and the problem of reality testing

Robert Wälder

Allow me first of all to ask your indulgence if in the remarks which I am about to make I do no more than suggest some fresh formulations bearing on facts which as such will be familiar to every analyst. To begin with, I should like to say at once, for the benefit of those in whom the title of this paper may have inspired a certain misgiving, that I have no intention of entering into any metaphysical discussions or of debating the problem of free will, which for centuries long has been the crux of philosophical systems; the problem to be investigated is the purely psychological one of freedom *from* something, for example, from affects or anxiety, or freedom *for* something, say freedom for coping with a task set before one. Anyone afflicted with an obsessional neurosis and acting under a compulsion is psychologically not free; if he is "freed" from his compulsion, he will have acquired a measure of freedom.

Rather than circumscribe my subject matter with elaborate definitions, I will try to take you at once to the heart of the matter with the help of some passages from Freud's writings, which will at the same time serve to show that this kind of problem has always occupied a focal position in psychoanalytic interest. Thus, for example, Freud says in reference to the development of the obsessional neurosis: "All these things combine to bring about an ever increasing indecisiveness, loss of energy, and curtailment of freedom."[1] In another passage we read: "Since the rules of analysis are diametrically opposed to the physician's making use of his personality in any such manner (as guide or prophet), it must be honestly confessed that here we have another limitation to the effectiveness of analysis; after all, analysis does not set out to abolish the possibility of morbid reactions, but to give the patient's ego *freedom* to choose one way or the other."[2] Or again: "It, too (the cultural superego), does not trouble enough about the mental constitution of human beings; it enjoins a command and never asks whether or not it is possible for them to obey it. It presumes, on the contrary, that a man's ego is psychologically capable of anything that is required of it —that his ego has unlimited power over his id. This is an error; even in so-called normal people the power of controlling the id cannot be increased beyond certain limits."[3]

If we have now given a sufficiently clear idea of our theme, we will take up our first question and consider in what consists the most general significance which we attach to the idea of freedom. Freedom in its most general sense seems to us to consist in a man appearing not to be tied down to his biological situation and to his environment,

---

[1] See *Introductory Lectures on Psycho-Analysis*, tr. by Joan Rivière (London: Allen and Unwin, 1936, p. 220; New York: Perma Giants, 1949).

[2] *The Ego and the Id*, tr. by Joan Rivière (London: Hogarth, 1927, p. 72; New York: W. W. Norton, 1962).

[3] *Civilisation and its Discontents*, tr. by Joan Rivière (London: Hogarth, 1930, p. 139; New York: W. W. Norton, 1961).

to the *hic et nunc* of his actual existence, but appearing to be able on occasion to pass beyond the actualities of his perceptual relations, to rise above himself and to objectify his standpoint of the moment. Thus it has been given to man to concern himself with and apprehend things which lie beyond the range not merely of his immediate perceptual relations but also of the paramount necessities of a given moment—as for instance you do, when you devote your attention to problems the treatment of which is certainly not a matter of immediate vital importance. In virtue of this freedom, man is able to make himself the subject matter of his own reflections, to objectify himself and to abstract himself from his own situation. The philosopher Georg Simmel has called this[4] "the transcendence of life," in accordance with the literal sense of the word *transcendere*: to step over, to place oneself above and beyond. A concrete manifestation of this is seen when a man, in virtue of his separate individuality, makes a will, thereby showing that he is aware that his life is limited, and from an imaginary vantage point beyond his transitory biological existence, as it were, is making dispositions for a time when he will have ceased to exist.

An array of facts, which time prevents me from entering into here, has inclined us to assume that in this transcendence, this rising above oneself, lies the essential difference between the nature of man and beast, that here and here alone we find the dimension which is missing from the life of the animals.[5]

These considerations, at first sight so far removed from

---

[4] See *Lebensanschauung* (Munich and Leipzig: Duncker und Humbolt, 1922).

[5] These facts include in the first instance the investigations made into the language of animals which have shown that their means of expression lacks a dimension, namely the function of representation, this being reserved to human speech, and that animal language

practical interests, have been applied in the field of pathology in elucidating neurological disturbances. Head, Gelb and Goldstein have traced a whole series of phenomena in the asymbolias, e.g., the so-called central aphasia, back to disturbances of just this dimension or stage in the development of human life; as when, for example, an aphasic subject is unable to find a certain word when he is asked for it to describe an object or situation, but has no difficulty in making use of identically the same word when in a specific vital situation he has need of it to express his state of mind; he is ready with words and gestures conveying

---

can only perform the tasks of expression and notification (K. Bühler). Further material is yielded by Wolfgang Köhler's observations on the difficulties encountered by the animals in his experiments over negative achievements; such tasks as involved, not imagining something (such as an implement) added to the environment optically perceived, but subtracting something from the field of vision, very soon brought them to grief. Of the same order, finally, is the circumstance that animals are without culture in the human sense. (Thus men concern themselves with the psychology of apes, but not apes with that of men.) In conclusion, we would refer to the impossibility of attributing to animals affects which presuppose a capacity to rise above oneself, such as irony and humor.

How the arrangement of organic life in grades is to be reconciled with the idea of evolution, whether there is a kind of uninterrupted process of transition from the animal stage to the human, what the position is with domesticated animals, are all questions which we cannot here submit even to the most cursory examination. A particularly noteworthy attempt to outline the development from the animal stage to the human has been made by G. Bally ("Die frühkindliche Motorik im Vergleich mit der Motorik der Tiere," *Imago*, Vol. XIX, 1933) in accordance with the sequence: biological retardation of development—prolonged care of the young—emancipation of functions from biological aims. The conceptual framework of Bally's work does not coincide completely with the formulations attempted here. But I must renounce the thought of discussing this now; I will only express my view that ultimately the two theories are identical or capable of being reduced to a common denominator.

threats and curses when he wants to threaten and curse, but remains silent and uncomprehending when one asks him for words and gestures conveying threats and curses.[6]

If now we translate this into the familiar idiom of our psychoanalytical terminology, we shall find that this rising above oneself, this self-scrutiny, self-appraisement and self-elimination which bring with them the possession of a world transcending an environment bound to perceptual and instinctual life, are a function of the superego, which we have long come to recognize as a grade in the ego. We know that in his superego man turns toward his own ego, sometimes attacking and punishing it, as in the phenomena of conscience, sometimes kindly and comforting, for instance, in humor, or again with emotional indifference, as when he observes himself and eliminates his personal standpoint. What is common to these modes of manifestation of the superego, their common factor, we might say, is the observation, objectification of one's self, the attainment of a position above one's own ego.[7] Permit me, if you will, to

[6] For the purposes of the conclusions to be drawn, it is not essential to accept the theories of Head and Goldstein in their entirety or to determine the extent of their sphere of application. It is quite enough that such disturbances exist: a circumstance taken into account by other theories as well.

[7] Although there exists a widespread usage in virtue of which the term "superego" is not infrequently applied as a synonym for "conscience," we should nevertheless remember that Freud originally introduced the ego ideal ("On Narcissism: An Introduction") in the light of the phenomena of delusions of observation, that is, as the institution of self-observation, and that even in his latest presentation of the tripartite structure of the psychic personality (*New Introductory Lectures on Psycho-Analysis*, p. 80) he states the problem in the light of the question "How can the ego take itself as object?" We therefore believe that we have not extended the psychoanalytical concept of the superego—although, had we done so, motives of expediency might perhaps have provided a justification—but that we have remained entirely at one with Freud's conception.

speak here of the formal function of the superego; its concrete content will be disregarded for the purposes of this investigation.

Freedom, then, in its most general sense is found in the existence of the superego, in that formal function of the superego in virtue of which man rises above himself and apprehends the world from without and beyond his immediate perceptions and his biological needs.

Now it would appear that there are three aspects of the problem of freedom: the formal function of his superego lifts man above things; at the same time, owing to his perceptions and affects he stands in their very midst, absorbed by them; but besides this, he finds himself face to face with them. We can therefore speak of a threefold freedom: its most general form which constitutes the essence of man, and is founded in the existence of the superego; a second form of which we may say provisionally and without strict regard to accuracy that the more he is "in the thick of it," the more he is in the grip of instincts and affects, the less this freedom is his; and thirdly, freedom to assess objects and reality as they are. Commensurate with these three aspects of freedom, we find a threefold derangement of it: the failure of the superego's function, over-absorption in affects, loss of freedom in relation to objects. These three disturbances or limitations of freedom seem to be realized in the three great realms of psychopathology: neurosis, psychosis, and asymbolia. In asymbolia, the formal function of the superego is apparently injured or eliminated; in neurosis man is overmuch absorbed by his instincts and affects, i.e. by fixations and anxiety; in psychosis, freedom is lacking in relation to objects. We see that this threefold stratification in the problem of freedom and its disturbances coincides in the main—although not wholly—with the tripartite division of the psychic personality with which analysis has made us familiar. Basing ourselves on our attempted formulations, we might add that asymbolia has its abode in the superego, neurosis in the id, and psychosis in the ego.

We will now proceed to consider the law which appears to hold in this sphere. Man is indeed able, in virtue of the formal function of his superego, to rise above himself, his impulses and his past, but he can do so only on certain conditions. A comparison will perhaps help to illustrate my meaning. When Archimedes discovered the laws of leverage, he exclaimed: "Only give me a fixed point in space and I will lift the world from its axes!" We, too, need to have a fixed point such as this if we are to lift the psychic structure from its axes, rise above our instinctual life and our past; a fixed point, however, located not in space, but in this mental life of ours itself, in our instinctual life and past. Thus man is able, it is true, to rise above his instinctual life (to overcome his fixations, for instance), but only if and in so far as he once more finds a fixed point in this his instinctual life and secures a foothold in his instinctual needs —as for example when he once more finds instinctual satisfaction in the very act of rising above himself; and he is able to vault beyond his past as it persists in his present life— if that were not possible, there would not be a psycho-analytical therapy—but he can only do so if and in so far as he regains his foothold in a past which really lives on. Accordingly we may say that man is able, in virtue of the formal function of his superego, to rise above his id, his instinctual life and the vicissitudes of his past, yet only if and in so far as he finds again in the id the Archimedean point which he needs. We see that the two axioms "man is free," and "man is not free" are both equally true and equally false. We are entitled to say that he is free, since he is always potentially capable of placing himself above and beyond the bonds of his historical and biological past.[8] We are entitled to say that he is not free, since he can only do this if at the same time he is able to secure a foothold in that past, and only to the extent to which he does so.[9]

It seems theoretically important to distinguish between plasticity—in a biological sense—and transcendence, raising oneself above oneself. We talk of plasticity in referring to the adaptation of a living being to a changing environment, when its experiences have not left an imprint so deep that that fact acts as a fixation for the experiences immediately following, and when its impulses readily find another object in place of one which has failed them. The psychical plasticity of a human being is at its height in early childhood and suffers a sharp decline with age; but the formation of grades in the ego gives rise to a process which is something

[8] The further elaboration of these theories would require us to distinguish between rising above something in a purely intellectual and in an experimental way (e.g., self-observation and humor). However we do not propose to pursue the question further within the limits of this paper.

[9] I have elsewhere attempted, using a different terminology, to hint at a formula to cover this same state of affairs ("Die latenten metaphysischen Grundlagen der psychologischen Schulen," I. Internationale Tagung für angewandte Psychopathologie und Psychologie, *Abhandlungen aus der Neurologie, Psychologie und Psychiatrie und ihren Grenzgebieten* LXI, (1931), 187 ff.). The philosophical influences at work in those formulations are there discussed in detail. I owe much to them for the phraseology employed; the facts themselves belong to psychoanalysis and were drawn from its field of experience. In psychoanalysis, R. Sterba ("The Fate of the Ego in Analytic Therapy," *International Journal of Psycho-Analysis*, XV, 1934) has been the first to adduce anthropological trains of thought following a suggestive passage from Herder. The present study has many points of contact with the lines of thought developed in that paper.

altogether different from the simple case in which the libido turns away from one object and is diverted to another; what happens is that an instinctual impulse is objectified, one rises above it—subject to the limitations imposed by the condition above discussed—and outgrows it, continuing the process at a higher level, so to say.

The former is a purely horizontal process, an impulse turns away from one object to another; the latter is, as it were, vertical, no longer simply a libidinal process, but one which passes through the superego.

L. von Krehl in his address[10] observes that, for instance, a number of people will scarcely trouble about a fish bone which is caught in their mouth, whereas in many the disturbing excitation evokes reactions of defense which grow more and more in intensity until finally the presence of the foreign body comes to dominate their whole existence and all their psychic energies are concentrated on its removal. There are people of great plasticity who pay little heed to a disturbing excitation of this kind; but if the disturbing excitation has released its reactions, if the plasticity of the organism has been inadequate, the excitation can no longer be mastered except in a second way; we are, of course, leaving out of account the removal of the foreign body, which is out of the question in the case of a psychic stimulus. If, then, plasticity has proved inadequate and fixation has taken possession of an individual, the only way which remains open is that of psychoanalysis.

But the distinction between plasticity and the attainment of a higher position, which in its turn is founded in instinctual satisfaction, is as a rule of as little significance for practice as it is important in theory. For the plasticity of instinctual life is also the basis on which the "vertical"

---

[10] L. von Krehl, *Krankheitsform und Persönlichkeit* (1929), p. 22.

function develops; the greater the plasticity of instinctual life, the more readily forthcoming will be the instinctual satisfaction necessary to help one to rise above one's fixations.

Our "law" also enables us to see in a particular light Freud's momentous notion of the secret propinquity of the superego to the instincts, perhaps the most daring in the whole field of psychoanalysis, and in any case the farthest removed from popular ideas and expectations. We find that that notion coincides exactly with what our attempted formulation leads us to anticipate: namely, that the attainment of a position above oneself from which one considers, praises or punishes one's own ego must in any case have secured a foothold in instinctual life, and that it is only with the support of instinct that one can put oneself above instinct.

This also enables us to understand how it happens that psychoanalysis is anxious to effect alterations in the id to further its therapeutic ends, but in doing so always addresses itself exclusively to the ego.

From this point of view, man appears, as he is revealed by psychoanalysis, a creature endowed with limited degrees of freedom; the limitations of freedom are the sites at which scientific psychology has made its colonies.[11] From here, a path opens out toward the differentiation of three fundamental types of pathological process. It is of little moment whether or not the types so discovered coincide completely with the empirical concepts of neurosis, psychosis, and asymbolia derived from clinical experience, as

---

[11] It cannot therefore be a coincidence that this scientific psychology originated as psychopathology, as the science of mental illnesses. We could in fact say that in the sphere of the central phenomena of personality there *could* only be a psychopathology.

little as it is necessary for the chemical elements to appear in a pure form in nature. The three types which we have separated out do not provide us with a key to the understanding of these three groups of illnesses, if only because we know that every illness, whether we are dealing with neurosis, psychosis or asymbolia is a process which passes through a course of development, and in which we find attempts to ward off the pathological process, attempts at assimilation, restitution, adaptation, and so forth. But we are inclined to think that along this path we may arrive at a means of setting up a system of coordinates in the realm of pathology, and that we do in fact find three distinct pathological processes corresponding to the three fundamental disorders at which we arrived, as it were, by way of deduction from the basic structure of the problem of freedom. Proceeding from the investigations of Head and Goldstein, we have already mentioned one of these fundamental disorders, namely the cessation of human freedom in its most general form, the disturbance of the function of the superego, the maintenance of man's animal tie, as we might call it, to the conditions of his existence. We can now find a more exact formula for neurotic disorder, which in a provisional and incomplete statement we defined as an over-great absorption in affects. In the neuroses, the subject does indeed rise above himself, the neurotic has insight into his illness and is able to take himself as the object of his reflections, but the Archimedean point never alters. His lack of freedom corresponds to the fixity of the props supporting his capacity for objectification. Lastly we find the third form of disturbance, that affecting freedom in relation to objects, in the psychoses.

It has to be admitted that this last subject has not yet been as fully elucidated as could be desired. The fact is that we understand the id and the superego better than we do the ego. From this third aspect of freedom and its disturbance a path leads us to the problem of the psychoses. The ego, or more correctly, its higher layers, issue from the two-sided situation between transcendence and absorption, between superego and id. We propose to select two examples from the higher functions of the ego which will demonstrate how far they really constitute the third co-ordinate; we refer to "intentional" activities and to causal thinking.

Man, as we have said, stands on the one hand above things, and on the other in their midst. It is in this double situation of being absorbed by and being above them that he comes to conceive objects "intentionally," as things that stand over against him; we regard this attitude as the third form of freedom. Now we know that a disturbance of volition is a characteristic of schizophrenia. A similar position obtains in relation to causal thinking, or, to put the matter in a more correct and generalized form, the "why" question. The existence of the superego gives us the category of possibility, enables us to conceive possibilities which are not realized. On the other hand, our perceptions and affective life keep us absorbed in reality. It is in this tension between reality and possibility that the question "why?" first originates.

We consider that we are entitled on quite general principles to distinguish two layers within that system which psychoanalysis has called the ego: those ego functions which we would assume to be present even in animals and which do not presuppose the existence of a superego, and those again which are modified by the presence and existence of the superego and the capacity derived from it to occupy a position above oneself. We would suggest that the one should be called the "animal ego" and the other the "human ego." The animal ego comprises the central control of the organism, which we may certainly assume comes very early into evidence in the animal kingdom, at latest with the appearance of the central nervous system; we may then attribute to the human ego those higher functions which would not be conceivable without the formal function of the superego, as for example the apprehending of objects "intentionally" or the "why" question, but also quite definitely the testing of reality.

The development of the higher layers of the ego (the "human ego") coincides with that of the superego, or of the formal function of the superego.

Perhaps this enables us to understand the reason for Freud's having at one time ascribed the function of reality testing to the superego and at another to the ego;[12] our investigation enables us to make the provisional statement that reality testing is a function of the ego, but belongs to those of the ego's functions which have been modified by the existence of the superego.

In all these higher acts of the ego which we ascribe to the human ego, we are able to distinguish an id component and a superego component, much as we tried to do when discussing "intentional" activities and the "why" question. Three simple illustrations may serve to clarify this statement.

The extent to which a man is approachable (in the everyday sense of the word, when we say that a man is or is not approachable) has an id and a superego aspect. The id aspect is represented by the amount of love which the individual in question entertains for his fellows and the way in which he deals with his aggression; the superego

---

[12] *Group Psychology and the Analysis of the Ego*, tr. by James Strachey (London: Hogarth, 1922; New York: W. W. Norton, 1961).

aspect is manifested in his readiness to abstract himself from his own standpoint and take over that of another, to put himself in the other man's shoes, as we are accustomed to say.

Similarly we can distinguish these two components in the process of reality testing. The id component consists in a man having a sufficient quantity of free object libido and his ego not being poisoned by narcissism; for we have learnt from Freud that always when libido has been withdrawn into the ego to any considerable extent so as to upset the equilibrium maintained between narcissism and object libido, manifestations of megalomania, the sexual overestimation of one's own ego, make their appearance and reality testing breaks down; just as an immoderate overflowing of the whole of the libido on to an object jeopardizes reality testing, although in a different manner. But, besides this, the id component is dependent on the distribution of Eros and aggressiveness; if a complete severance has occurred between them so that all erotic strivings are concentrated on a single person or group of persons and all aggressive ones on the rest of mankind, the reality testing will suffer, since it is impossible to see clearly any more where one feels only love or only hate. The superego component in the testing of reality consists in man's distinguishing, in virtue of his capacity for self-observation, between inner and outer, between reality and fantasy.[13] Thus disturbances in all these higher acts of the

---

[13] I have discussed these questions in greater detail elsewhere: "Lettre sur l'étiologie et l'évolution des psychoses collectives suivie de quelques remarques sociologiques concernant la situation historique actuelle" (*Publications de l'Institut International de Coopération Intellectuelle*, Coll. Correspondance, Vol. III, Chapter VI (1934): "Atteintes portées a l'épreuve de la réalité," pp. 107 ff.)

ego may issue from two directions, from the id as well as from the superego.[14]

As our third and last example we may refer to the fact of communication or confession; Reik's writings[15] have long made us familiar with its superego aspect, the compulsion to confess under the pressure of the sense of guilt; recently a paper by Dorothy Burlingham[16] has revealed to us its id aspect in exhibitionism and attempts at seduction.

These provisional examples may serve to demonstrate, if only incompletely, that the position of the "human ego" is that occupied by those layers of the ego which, supported by the id, develop in an individual who has a superego, and disturbances in which help to populate the third province of psychopathology, that of the psychosis.

We could still try to add a number of equivalents to the formulations already attempted for the three principal types of pathological process which we have represented in terms of the three conceivable forms of disturbance of freedom. We will here only suggest one: the category of the possible is absent in asymbolia, the neurotic is over-absorbed by reality—and here reality includes fantasy, psychical reality—and the psychotic fails to distinguish between reality and possibility.

Let us try to clarify the three principal types of pathological process by means of a schematic example. Let us proceed from the simple hypothesis that someone has lost a loved object through death and then ask ourselves which will be the appropriate reactions of each of the three types.

---

[14] This can also be seen in the pathological field: psychotic manifestations can appear as well following on neurological disturbances as on instinctual outbursts.

[15] Reik, *Geständniszwang und Strafbedürfnis* (Leipzig and Vienna: International Psychoanalytic Library, 1925).

[16] Dorothy Tiffany Burlingham, "Mitteilungsdrang und Geständniszwang," *Imago*, XX (1934).

The aphasic patient will perhaps no longer be able to utter or comprehend the namc of the lost object; for him the world extends no farther than the horizon of his immediate perceptions, his mind no longer reaches beyond them; unless a place can be found for it here, a thing ceases to exist. He has lost the category of the possible, his existence is confined to his actual environment at a given moment and to what his vital needs turn his attention.

The neurotic may react with a protracted period of mourning or will perhaps develop a symptom which will allow the dead to survive in a psychical reality expressive of his longing, or with feelings of guilt and so forth. The neurotic has at his disposal the category of the possible, but he is absorbed by a part of his affective life, by pain, longing, or a sense of guilt. Here we see that every gradation exists between neurotic and normal. In this theoretical sense, even normal reactions of mourning can be described as a minor neurosis.

Lastly the psychotic will perhaps develop a delusion that the dead person is still alive or will hallucinate his presence. He also has at his disposal the category of the possible. He has not, as in asymbolia, reduced the world to the dimensions of his immediate surroundings and instinctual needs. The function of his superego is still maintained. Like the neurotic, he remains absorbed by affects, but he no longer distinguishes reality from possibility, he mistakes a part of the world of possibility for reality. Accordingly his disorder is related to the higher functions of the ego.

This example[17] also shows us how fully we are entitled

---

[17] We see moreover where it is inadequate: what the asymboliac subject in our example fails to transcend (namely, the perceptual situation) is not the same thing as what absorbs the neurotic (namely, the affect). Whether this amounts simply to a flaw in the example itself or whether it betrays an as yet unresolved difficulty running through the whole argument must be left undecided.

in all three cases to speak of a curtailment of freedom. The aphasic subject's loss of freedom consists in his becoming enslaved to the things of his immediate surroundings and to current actualities, and in his no longer retaining that freedom to break away from his perceptions and the actual moment which is the most universal feature distinguishing human beings. The neurotic in his mourning reaction or the torments of his longing and feelings of guilt enjoys this species of freedom, but he stands in the shadow of his affects and lacks the freedom to choose a point in the life of his emotions which could help him to rise above the remainder of his affects. The psychotic, lastly, has also not sacrificed the most universal form of human freedom, but he lacks freedom to apprehend things as they really are.[18]

---

[18] If a loose conjecture may be allowed us here, we would express a surmise that there are also three biological processes corresponding to these three principal types. Absorption in instincts and affects has a corollary in modifications in the chemical substances—a very early anticipation of Freud's which recent work in the investigation of hormones seems to corroborate; we know that the asymbolias arise from injury to the cerebral cortex, that is, from injuries to what are phylogenetically the most recent parts of the central nervous system. The correspondence between the more peripheral changes concerned in sexual chemistry and what we have described as absorption in affects is only too obvious; whereas we are, of course, still completely in the dark as to the biological process which corresponds to the psychoses. It would be much too crude and misleading to base an analogy on this— peripheral disturbances in sexual chemistry, central disturbances in the phylogenetically most recent parts of the central nervous system—and then to conclude that here we have before us disturbances of the phylogenetically older parts of the central nervous system. Besides many other factors, the problem is complicated by the law in virtue of which, in the higher animals, functions are transferred to the phylogenetically more recent parts of the central nervous system; even functions of a lowly order are, in the higher animals, regulated by higher organizations of the central nervous system. This law accords well with our psychological conception

From the considerations which I have so far allowed myself to submit to your judgment a further line of thought carries us on to the problem of ego expansion and ego limitation. Let us recall Freud's dictum: "Where id was, there shall ego be."[19] We conceive this expansion of the ego as an increase in freedom, indeed in that form of freedom which we found to have suffered detriment in the neuroses: freedom from absorption in one's instincts and affects, freedom to choose the Archimedean point in order to rise above oneself. The way in which this comes about and is constantly being realized in psychoanalytical therapy has, we think, been delineated in the "law" which we have already formulated, namely that a man rises above his id if and in so far as he finds the Archimedean point in his id once more. The problem of ego limitation mooted by Anna Freud[20] is also relevant here. Anna Freud described among the variety of forms which the mastery of anxiety assumes in the child, one which consists in withdrawing from the danger zone, in renouncing and abandoning activities which bring it into jeopardy. In that case freedom from anxiety is purchased at the expense of a limitation of the

---

of a modification of the ego (the human ego) through the existence of the superego. We should certainly expect to find not a simple localized cleavage, but a severance between acts and modes of function. As, however, we already appear to have found analogies for at any rate two dimensions, it is perhaps not vain to hope that we shall one day discover them for the third; or more correctly, for the third and fourth, seeing that human and animal components of the ego may very well correspond to different forms of organization of the central nervous system.

[19] *New Introductory Lectures on Psycho-Analysis*, tr. by W. J. Sprott (London: Hogarth, 1933, p. 106; New York: W. W. Norton, 1933. Paper edition, 1962).

[20] Paper read before the Twelfth International Psycho-Analytical Congress, Wiesbaden, 1932.

ego. A permanent curtailment of freedom has been effected, has become as it were—*sit venia verbo*—character.

Before we are in a position to subject to a more accurate analysis the problem thus raised of ego strength and ego limitation, it is important to distinguish real strength of the ego from what we might describe as a pseudo strength of the ego, which when seen from the outside often presents a very similar appearance. An instance of this pseudo strength of the ego would be when the fear of being thought a coward is stronger than the fear of danger. Certain recent tendencies in education which aim at allowing the child a greater measure of freedom during the latency period lead, as Anna Freud has shown, to the child's withdrawing under the pressure of its anxiety from activities which bring it into danger, and consequently to a limitation of its ego. In certain of the more antiquated forms of education which even now find favor in many circles, this way was closed to the child, since cowardice was utterly condemned and feared even more than danger. Under conditions such as these, the ego does not suffer a limitation, yet what remains is not a strong ego, although, it may sometimes appear to resemble this; we would call it a pseudo strength of the ego.

We find a second instance of pseudo strength of the ego when, for example, infantile omnipotence fantasies persist in part, when the belief in omnipotence has found confirmation in reality for some reason or other at a time so early that thenceforward it has in general remained within the confines of reality, and not overstepped the borderline of psychosis.[21]

Real ego strength, on the other hand, seems to consist

---

[21] On this process, see H. Nunberg, *Allgemeine Neurosenlehre* (Berlin: H. Huber, 1932), p. 277 ff.

in the capacity to rise constantly above one's instincts and affects and—this is the crux of the matter—to apply the Archimedean lever at any number of different points in one's own id.[22] This gives to the ego a measure of real freedom, all that man with the inherent limits upon his freedom is able to achieve. Here we again come across a point to which we tried to allude before in passing, namely that plasticity also forms the basis for the "vertical" process of raising oneself above an instinct with the help of an instinct. This rather suggests to us that the antithesis of a strong ego may be found in the adhesiveness of the libido.

In conclusion, we propose to consider a few tentative applications of the point of view which we have here presented.

The difference which exists between our attitude in social relationships and a pedagogic or therapeutic attitude amounts to this, that in the former we treat our fellow men as if they were completely free; we make demands, appraise and condemn. As pedagogues and therapists we treat the other party, or, more correctly, the object of our pedagogical or therapeutic activity, as one who is not free; or, to be more precise, as though his freedom were limited in the several ways we have described. Why indeed this should be the case, why man's social relationships require

---

[22] When one rises above an impulse with the support of the *same* impulse, we call it "sublimation." The word describes the process and its result. This definition differs from the usual one (diversion of the impulse to other, more valuable aims) as a "vertical" description of the process, which takes into account the structural stratification, as distinguished from a purely "horizontal" one. It seeks at the same time to do justice to Freud's dictum that sublimation takes place regularly through the mediation of the ego (*The Ego and the Id*, London: Hogarth, 1927, p. 64) and may help us to understand why a repressed impulse is not capable of being sublimated.

him to treat others as though their conduct were entirely free—failing this, the social relation is disturbed—would need a separate investigation.

A further application takes us to the problem of predicting human action and human conduct. Fundamentally it is only possible to do this if and in so far as freedom exists only to a limited degree. Accordingly we can predict an individual's conduct most surely where we have to do with the most extreme form of limitation affecting freedom—in asymbolia. Goldstein declares that he does not conclude his investigation of a patient until he is able to forecast with certainty his reactions to any given situation. The probable correctness of a prediction concerning the future behavior of a psychotic is already slighter, but predictions exist here as well, they go by the name of psychiatric prognoses, which we know to be subject to considerable uncertainties. Lastly, in the case of the neurotic, the probability is one degree more uncertain still; the probable correctness of a prediction will be further reduced. In fact it is only possible to make predictions at all in so far as limitations on freedom are present; but since these limitations are necessarily present in every human being—the differences between neurotic and normal are, as we see here, only a matter of degree—it is possible in some sense to make predictions even in the sphere of normal psychology. In brief, we may say that the greater the limitation on freedom, the more probably correct prediction will be.

This last point is also, we think, relevant to the question of founding a scientific sociology, the aim of which is to lay down general propositions concerning human conduct, in the last resort based on psychology. In one direction, the task of sociology is facilitated by the existence of a field, over and above the sphere already discussed of maximal limitations on freedom, in which it is possible to predict human behavior with a degree of probability approximating to certainty, at least in the sense of a statistical mean: namely, the field of individuo-peripheral manifestations. We say of a process that it is individuo-peripheral if it is unaccompanied by internal conflict, as in the case of the satisfaction of needs which are more or less common to all men and approved by the superego, and if the means employed in obtaining this satisfaction are known and legitimate. Thus we can predict that people will prefer a cheaper market if they can obtain the same commodities with the same psychical satisfaction at a smaller sacrifice. This is not a case of limitation upon freedom, but an individuo-peripheral activity—no conflict arises. Behavior such as this can also be predicted. This fact is at the basis on the one hand of a large part of non-analytical psychology, in so far as this has been stated in laws, and, on the other, of the possibility of political economy as the only body of scientific laws within the domain of the social sciences.

We will, however, abandon this survey of the field of applied psychology in favor of a return to our proper theme, and in conclusion cast a few side lights on the problems of the transformations of freedom during the course of man's life, of psychoanalytic therapy and of the theoretical bases of psychoanalytic pedagogy.

How then does freedom, as we have sought to describe it, develop throughout the course of man's span of life? Are we here dealing with a constant quantity or with a process of average regularity? We consider that two curves are here superimposed one upon the other. On the one hand, man only gradually awakens to the freedom which has been given him. The superego is not there from the very first day, the formal function of the superego likewise fails to appear in the reactions of the suckling, and even when that function has become visible in behavior and in the obtaining of mastery over things, it has still far to go before reaching its zenith. A variety of experiences has taught us that the child only very gradually comes to acquire a certain degree of relativism, that he finds it extremely difficult even during his latency period to eliminate his own standpoint and recognize its subjective nature, and that it requires maturity in order to objectify permanently one's destiny and actual situation.[23] Finally humor, the finest flower of the superego, seems to be a prerogative of more advanced years.[24] Accordingly we may speak of a development of the function of the superego, or of man's gradual awakening to that kind of freedom which we have described as its most general form.

But this rising curve has a counterpart in another, declining one. Every day of our experience leaves behind irrevocable traces which tend to limit our freedom. I refer in part to external matters—love, marriage and a career

---

[23] Naturally this is not to say that self-observation is in all its forms an ideal thing. Self-objectification has its pathological forms as well; as when for example the obsessional type (in the sense of Freud's libidinal types) becomes, in the pathologically exaggerated form of obsessional neurosis, the spectator and reporter of his own experience. (Cf. in this connection Fenichel, *Hysterie, Phobie und Zwangsneurose*, Vienna: Internationaler psychoanalytischer Verlag, 1931, p. 150 ff.). Relevant to this phenomenon is the question which we mentioned earlier, as falling outside the scope of this paper, of an intellectual and experimental rising above something; and in addition, there is the fact that it is always a part only of experience which is so observed—the other part is repressed and so shut out from the field of view accessible to self-observation.

[24] Cf. E. Kris, "Zur Psychologie der Karikatur," *Imago*, XX (1934), p. 465 ff.

create conditions which mark out a framework for later life—in part to internal matters, in the sense that the experience of each day turns some of the potentialities latent in the individual into reality, and thus causes a limitation of his possibilities; each day represents, as it were, a partial fixation involving a limitation of freedom in regard to his later life.

The superimposition of these two curves seems to determine the curve of human life, which coincides in its course with the biological one—again clearly not a coincidence— leading upwards to begin with until it reaches its culminating point, at which it remains for a time, and then finally declining. On the upward gradient, awakening to one's possibilities still outweighs the twofold limitation imposed on freedom by the increasing demands of external reality and by growing fixation. The horizontal section corresponds to the maximum individual freedom to which man is able to attain within the conditions prescribed for him by his constitution, his past history and his environment, and so far as circumstances or illness permit. The downward slope shows where man becomes more and more the petrified image of his past.

A further application, finally, brings us to the problem of psychoanalytic therapy. Various forms of therapeutic influence are known to medical science, such as eliminating the point at which the pathological process has set in (for instance, an operation for the removal of diseased tissue), reinforcing the organism's powers of resistance, or lastly the implantation of another biological process (e.g. transplantation). Psychoanalysis comes forward as an appeal to man's freedom itself—to such freedom as is his, of course, and so far as it is his, to the limited but none the less existing degree of human freedom—and in this way it serves not only to overcome illness, but also to strengthen the ego and to augment freedom. Psychoanalytic therapy thus in any case stands nearer to the therapeutic ideal than any other method of cure known to medicine. The distinction between the psychoanalytic and other psychotherapeutic procedures is found to be similar to that which in our earlier formulation we tried to draw between a real strength and a pseudo strength of the ego; these latter procedures do not extend human freedom, but interpolate a new determinism and create a fresh situation of absorption (e.g., by means of an unregulated transference on to the physician). A satisfactory result may be obtained if the sole object has been the removal of a symptom; just as the teacher who wishes his pupil to be good at sport may feel satisfied if fear of being a coward restrains the boy from flight from the danger zone. But it is certainly not therapy in the strict sense of the term.[25]

From here we can also discern the limits of psycho-analytic therapy. All that we have long known empirically concerning these may be arrived at by way of deduction from our scheme; as for example the fact that the therapeutic prospects of analysis depend not so much on the severity of the neurosis as on a part of the personality having remained intact, and the extent of this. One point more than any deserves mention: the degree of freedom which an individual enjoys consists not in his being granted certain kinds of freedom and denied others, but in the circumstance that there is a contradistinction between absorption in the

---

[25] We have thus reached by another route the same distinction between the psychoanalytic and other forms of therapy as Rado gave in his paper "The Economic Principle in Psycho-Analytic Technique," *International Journal of Psycho-Analysis*, Vol. VI, 1925.

totality of one's affects and rising in a fundamental sense above everything. We have already said that the two axioms "man is free" and "man is not free" are equally true and equally false. Perhaps this will also explain how it happens that psychoanalytic therapy can at one moment convey the impression that a man has completely changed and at another that he has at bottom remained the same. In this favorable instance of a successful therapeutic treatment, he has become a completely different man, for he has risen above his instincts, affects, habits and morbid reactions. He has remained quite unchanged, for he has at the same time found once more a foothold in this his psychic nature and in his past history.[26]

In conclusion, we consider that proceeding from the

---

[26] The American poet-philosopher George Santayana, in his book *Dialogues in Limbo* (New York, 1926), makes a sage in the underworld speak of a book entitled "The Wheel of Ignorance and the Lamp of Knowledge." The wheel of ignorance would have the world based on a number of principles, regarded numerically, like the spokes of a wheel; the correct view sees in these principles points of view which illuminate things first from one side and then from another, like a lamp swinging in space, shedding its cones of light upon things. ("My benefactor has entitled his profound work 'The Wheel of Ignorance and the Lamp of Knowledge'; because, he said, the Philosopher having distinguished four principles in the understanding of nature, the ignorant conceive these principles as if they were the four quadrants of a wheel, on any one of which in turn the revolving edifice of nature may be supported; whereas wisdom would rather have likened those principles to the four rays of a lamp suspended in the midst of the universe from the finger of Allah, and turning on its chain now to the right and now to the left; whereby its four rays, which are of divers colors, lend to all things first one hue and then another without confusing and displacing anything.") This poetical comparison may serve as an illustration to show that we have not here set freedom and the lack of it side by side as materially distinct sectors.

ideas here discussed an attempt could be made to outline the theoretical bases of psychoanalytical pedagogy. Every pre-analytical pedagogy recognizes two ways of influencing the child. One of them is training, associating one kind of conduct with pleasure and another with "pain," the method of rewards and punishments; at bottom, it is the same method as is applied by the animal psychologist when in a maze experiment he trains the animal by means of electric shocks to follow a particular direction. The other method consists in holding up to the child an ideal, a hortative "shall." The first method estimates the freedom of its object as practically nonexistent, the second, as unlimited. The first method is animal and subhuman, the second divine and superhuman. Thus non-analytical psychology oscillates between a method proper to animals and another proper to God, but loses sight of one adapted to men. In contradistinction to these, psychoanalytical pedagogy represents a beginning of a human pedagogy. It regards its object as a creature endowed with a measure, albeit a limited measure, of freedom, takes into consideration the lack of freedom or the limitations on freedom present at the time, and tries to work with such freedom as is available and gradually to extend it.

This paper was first read before the Thirteenth International Psycho-Analytical Congress in Lucerne on August 28, 1934. It was published in *Imago*, Vol. XX, 1934 under the title "Das Freiheitsproblem in der Psychoanalyse und das Problem der Realitätsprüfung." It later appeared in the *International Journal of Psycho-Analysis*, Vol. XVII, 1936, in English. The translator is unknown.

Robert Wälder was trained in psychoanalysis in Vienna during the movement's early days. He has written extensively on the relationship of psychoanalysis to art.

Development of the ego psychology

Franz Alexander

The structural and dynamic approach to the actually observed mental processes has in the last ten years undergone
a rapid development. From 1921 on we can speak of the
evolution of a new analytic ego psychology. A deeper investigation of the fundamental processes of repression was
the starting point of this new development. The central
problem became: which psychic factors are responsible for
repression and how does this process take place in detail?
It soon became evident that fear is the motive power behind
all repression. Characteristic of this fear, however, is the
fact that it is by no means a rational or entirely conscious
fear of external and actual danger, but an inner fear which
appears in consciousness as a guilty conscience. This phenomenon is most satisfactorily described by saying that one
part of the personality exhibits fear of another part, which
in ordinary language is called conscience, and that repression serves to avert this fear reaction. In other words, those
mental tendencies, wishes, longings, ideas, are excluded
from the conscious personality as would arouse self-con-
demnation if they entered consciousness, for this self-
condemnation is associated with fear like that experienced

in the face of real danger. The historical investigation of the repressed tendencies has shown that those are apt to arouse a guilt conflict which at some previous time, usually in infancy, had actually caused the individual pain, parental punishment, or contempt. The fear of the parents thus becomes embodied in the fear of one's own conscience. The assumption was inevitable that during development a part of the personality assumes the attitude, opinions, and judgments of persons in authority, usually of the parents, and this embodiment of the parents now assumes the same attitude toward the rest of the personality as the parents previously manifested toward the child. This process of identification with the parents and the incorporation of their image into the mental apparatus is the process which we usually call adjustment to the social environment. One part of the personality accepts the code of education and becomes a representative of the demands of society, and this part Freud called the superego. It is important to realize that not the whole of the personality participates in social adjustment and that even in normal persons there is a steady and permanent tension between the original, non-adjusted, instinctual tendencies, and the restrictive influence of the superego.

The existence of the superego explains how in every form of civilization there is a self-regulating or self-restrictive force in individuals which is indispensable for social order. If an internal code of law such as the superego or, to use the more popular expression, the conscience, were not present, social order could only be secured by assigning to every citizen a policeman to make him conform with accepted social behavior. Social behavior is by no means enforced only by fear of external punishment; there is also in every adjusted individual a restrictive force, which in the course of development becomes more or less independent of external reinforcement, such as admonition and threats of punishment. On the other hand, it also became evident in the light of psychological analysis that the inner assimilation of social prescriptions is limited to only a few, very fundamental regulations. Without fear of punishment, the majority of people would behave less socially than they actually do, for the superego does not entirely replace real persons in authority.

The only way to test empirically which nonsocial tendencies are controlled by the internal restricting functions of the superego and those which must still be controlled by a police force would be to make the impossible experiment of abolishing all punishments. A statistical investigation as to what kinds of crime and unsocial behavior increase under these circumstances and what criminal tendencies no longer need external control would furnish a criterion of the degree to which the man of today is essentially adjusted to the requirements of collective life. From psychoanalytic experience it could be predicted with some degree of probability that in our present civilization only cannibalism, actual incest, parricide, and fratricide would not increase, even if there were no punishment for these crimes in the penal code. These nonsocial tendencies, though manifest at the beginning of man's development, are repressed in contemporary civilization so successfully, that there is no danger of their actual realization. Cannibalism, for example, no longer needs the special prohibitions necessary in some primitive civilizations, for it is deeply repressed, although unquestionably existent at the beginning of everyone's development.

Whereas the normal individual is able to domesticate and modify his unsocial, instinctual tendencies, the psychoneurotic remains more firmly fixated to them. The way which the neurotic chooses for the solution of his conflict between repressing and repressed non-adjusted mental forces is a substitution of fantasy for the actual realization of his wishes, though not even in his fantasy can he express directly his non-adjusted tendencies, since the conscious, adjusted portion of his personality denies their existence.

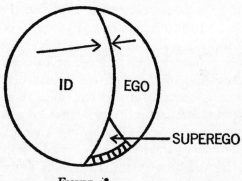

FIGURE 1*

The shaded portion of the section, which represents the superego, expresses the fact that the superego in a fully developed personality has lost its connection with external reality. It is more or less rigid and has sunk to the depth of the personality. It is consequently to a high degree unconscious.[1]

---

[1] In my book, *The Psychoanalysis of the Total Personality* (New York and Washington: Nervous and Mental Diseases Publishing Co., 1930), I proposed a distinction between the entirely unconscious superego and the conscious ego ideal. The latter contains those specific values acquired in later life and which are the conscious directing forces of conduct. This distinction was accepted by many psychoanalysts, but it seems to me questionable whether one should consider the ego ideal more closely connected with the superego, as its continuation in the consciousness, or more allied to the actual ego. This could be expressed by Figure 2.

* All diagrams in this article by courtesy of W. W. Norton & Co.

The outcome is a disguised fantastic expression of them in psychoneurotic symptoms.

Furthermore, the investigation of dreams has shown that even in normal persons unconscious remnants of nonsocial tendencies are at work, for the often unintelligible and senseless dreams of adults are disguised expressions of tendencies rejected by the adjusted part of the personality. Consequently dreams can be considered the neurotic symptoms of normal persons. In any case the dynamic basis of dream formation is identical with that of neurotic symptom formation and, in fact, the technique of dream analysis has proven to be the most delicate instrument for the investigation of the dynamic interplay of repressed and repressing mental forces. This microscopic research into symptom and dream formation has led to a kind of stereopsychology, for it has developed a concept of the structure of personality and has reconstructed intrapsychic processes which go on between the structurally differentiated parts of the personality. We can distinguish three structurally differentiated parts of the mental apparatus:

1. The inherited reservoir of chaotic, instinctual demands which are not yet in harmony with each other nor with the facts of external reality is called, on account of its impersonal quality, the id. 2. The ego is the integrating part of the personality which modifies and, by a process of selection and control, brings the original tendencies of the id into harmony, excluding those the realization of which would occasion conflict with external reality. 3. Finally, the third part of the mental apparatus, the result of the latest adjustment, is the superego which embodies the code of society. Naturally this code is dependent upon the social environment and differs according to the cultural milieu in which the individual was brought up.

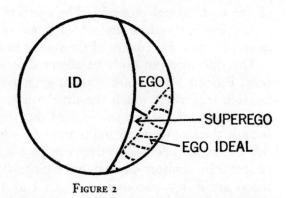

FIGURE 2

The dotted line expresses the fact that the ego ideal is not a completely separate unit, since it is hard to differentiate between conscious values, ideals, guiding principles and the rest of the ego. On the other hand, it is also difficult to make a sharp distinction between the entirely unconscious, almost automatic influences of the superego and those more or less conscious ones which direct our decisions and general conduct.

It may sound paradoxical that our knowledge of the conscious ego is far behind what we know about the nature and functions of the id, and especially of the superego. It sounds paradoxical because the ego is the part of personality of which we are constantly aware, and is the part which we think we know and feel as our actual personality. Perhaps, however, just this nearness to it is one of the reasons which makes its scientific investigation so difficult. The difficulty of understanding the ego with the help of the ego was expressed in older philosophical treatises by such metaphors as "It is impossible to cut a knife with a knife." Psychoanalysis, however, is not an introspective method, although it has to utilize introspection in understanding the personalities of others, because in psychology the presupposition of all such understanding of others is a knowledge of our own mental processes. The nearness to one's own personality is therefore undoubtedly one of the obstacles to an objective description of the functions of the ego.

This difficulty can easily be observed in clinical experience. Patients often admit without great resistance objectionable tendencies which the psychoanalyst shows them are in their unconscious and outside their actual ego. Just because these condemned and repressed tendencies are outside the actual personality they can be admitted, and the patient can comfort himself by saying: "These strange things are in my unconscious, but not in me, i.e., not in the part of my personality which I feel to be my ego." The real conflict arises only after the unconscious tendencies begin to enter the ego and the patient begins to feel them as part of his actual personality.

Another reason that it seems paradoxical for our knowledge of the ego to be less advanced than that of the unconscious parts of the personality, is that the ego is far more complicated and advanced in development than the id, which is a reservoir of the primary forces, or than the superego, which is a kind of complex of highly differentiated conditioned reflexes and reflex inhibitions.

What can be said with certainty about the ego is that it is a formation of two perceptive surfaces, one directed toward the instinctual life (inner perception), the second directed toward external reality (sense perception). One main function of the ego is to confront the facts of inner perception with the results of sense perception, i.e., to bring subjective demands in harmony with the external circumstances. Its tendency is to find satisfaction for as many of the subjective needs and wishes as possible under existing external circumstances. The conscious ego is the most plastic part of the mental apparatus, since it can adjust the behavior at any moment to a given situation, in contrast to reflex and automatic behavior which is fixed and predetermined in a much higher degree. Automatic reactions are rigid and adjusted to certain stimuli, and so cannot adjust themselves to a sudden change in the external situation, whereas the ego has the capacity of performing adjustments of *ad hoc*.

The functioning of the whole mental apparatus can be described approximately as follows: Instinctual needs and tendencies arising in the id tend to become conscious because the conscious ego controls the motor innervations on which the satisfaction of the needs is dependent. A great part of the instinctual demands becomes immediately conscious and finds its acceptance or rejection after a process of conscious deliberation. This deliberation involves an estimate of the external situation and a comparison of the inner demand in question with other conflicting tendencies present in consciousness. For example, if someone had to decide whether he really wanted to attend a lecture or go to a theater, there would be a conscious conflict which could be solved by a conscious judgment. Such tendencies and conflicts, however, have nothing whatever to do with repression. In such a case one desire is abandoned because it is incompatible with another more important. Repression, however, is a function which excludes certain tendencies from becoming conscious. It only occurs in cases in which the mere existence of a wish, irrespective of its realization, would cause an unbearable conscious conflict. To mention only one typical example, hostile feelings against a benefactor would tend to be repressed because they destroy our good opinion of ourselves. Similar non-

CONSCIOUS CONFLICT

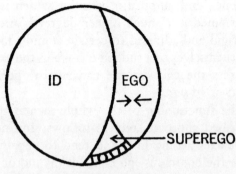

UNCONSCIOUS CONFLICT

FIGURE 3

social tendencies, to which the susceptibility of different individuals varies on account of the differences in their infantile experience, are inhibited even before they can become conscious. Repression, in contrast to conscious rejection, is a process of inhibition which arises on a deeper level of personality—somewhere on the borderline between id and ego—and saves the conscious personality from becoming aware of a painful conflict.

It is obvious that such an unconscious inhibiting process presupposes a kind of unconscious inner perception which leads to automatic, almost reflex inhibitions, similar to a conditioned reflex. This unconscious censoring function we ascribe to the superego. Repression is consequently based on a kind of unconscious censorship which reacts automatically to unacceptable tendencies. Although this process appears to us as a kind of unconscious selective judgment, which excludes certain definite tendencies from consciousness, nevertheless we have to assume that it operates schematically, is incapable of subtle differentiation, and reacts uniformly to certain emotional factors in spite of their actual and sometimes important differences. It is comparable with a conditioned reflex rather than with a deliberate judgment. To cite a trivial example, the repression of the first incestuously tinged sexual strivings of the child establishes a general pattern of sexual repression which persists in later life, so that at the reawakening of sexuality in adolescence, there is a general timidity and inhibition. The sexual impulse, although it has now lost its manifestly incestuous character and is directed to acceptable exogamous objects, suffers from the intimidations of the childhood. The superego lacks the capacity of making finer distinctions, and represses sexuality in general without being able to recognize that the object of striving is no longer the same as in childhood. The well-known picture of the adolescent as shy and inhibited shows the result of this automatic process of restriction. In short, repression is always exaggerated and involves tendencies which the conscious ego would not reject if they became conscious. This important automatic and over-severe inhibiting function of the superego appears as one of the most general causes of psychoneurotic disturbances. Psychoneurotic symptoms are the dynamic results of unbearable tensions occasioned by the weight of exaggerated repressions.

Let us now describe the act of repression more fully. It starts with the superego's inner perception of a dynamic tension which tends to become conscious in order to induce the motor innervations necessary for its release. If the tendency is in conflict with the code of the superego, the conscious ego rejects it from fear, which is the motive power of repression. The ego, acting on the cue given by the superego, rejects the condemned id tendency, and so produces what we call repression. The fear felt by the ego for the superego is the signal which warns the ego to repress, and this intimidation of the ego by the superego can be considered as the continuation of the pressure which the parents brought to bear upon the child during the period of education.

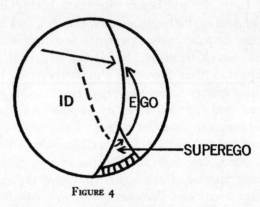

FIGURE 4

The dotted line represents the inner perception of the repressed tendency by the superego. Repression is like a reflex arc consisting of a sensory and a motor part. The dotted line represents the sensory part, the arrow starting in the section, superego, and continued in the ego, the motor part. Repression is an automatic or reflectory inhibition.

The ego is exposed to two directing forces: the individual needs arising from the id, on the one hand, and their denial by the superego on the other. Its tendency is to compromise between the two forces by modifying the id tendencies in a way which is compatible with the code of the superego. This process we call domestication, or sublimation of the original, inherited, nonsocial demands.

Sublimation is what occurs in normal adjustment. The neurotic and psychotic personality is characterized by a relatively small capacity for sublimation.[2] These pathological personalities stubbornly hold on to their original tendencies, which they cannot carry out because, paradoxically enough, they have at the same time developed a harsh superego. They are both over-social and nonsocial at the same time.

---

[2] The *absolute* rate of the capacity for sublimation may in certain cases of neurosis be great, but then the inhibition of unsublimated gratifications makes the need for sublimations greater than the neurotic is able to perform—hence the production of symptoms.

This article first appeared in the *International Journal of Psycho-Analysis*, Vol. XIII, 1932. It was reprinted in *Psychoanalysis Today*, edited by Sandor Lorand (New York: Covici-Friede, 1933), and later in another edition of this volume (New York: International Universities Press, 1944).

Franz Alexander is considered one of the foremost post-Freudian theorists. Well-known for his interest in and development of ego psychology, he has a wide following among psychoanalysts here and abroad.

A discussion of certain forms of resistance

Helene Deutsch

The subject of defense mechanisms, which was first opened up by Freud in his *Inhibitions, Symptoms and Anxiety* (1926), has received a further expansion and clarification in Anna Freud's recent book.[1] It will undoubtedly give a stimulus to further investigations in the same field.

The analyst has an opportunity during treatment of studying the mechanisms of defense in their purest form. He meets with them under the aspect of resistance, i.e., in the functions which ward off or weaken the psychical tendencies mobilized by the analysis. Confronted with defense mechanisms which function well and perform positive services to the ego, psychoanalytical treatment has only one task: that of strengthening them, in so far as they do not function as a resistance against repressed material which is important for the ego.

It is obvious to all of us that the resistances which we encounter as an "anti-cathexis" will have a particular character appropriate to each form of neurosis and to each analytic situation. Nevertheless it seems worth while to

[1] *The Ego and the Mechanisms of Defence* (New York: International Universities Press, 1948).

attempt to bring about a certain grouping and order in this mass of self-evident material.

To begin with, it is, in spite of everything, not entirely clear why in certain individuals one type and in others another type of defense stands in the foreground, and why, although other forms of defense are simultaneously present, the analytic situation is predominantly colored by some particular defensive tendency.

I have attempted, first and foremost, to arrange the typical forms of resistance in three groups, corresponding to the three chief currents which together constitute the essence of analytical technique, and to subdivide these in turn into typical subgroups and lastly to investigate them in relation to their origin.

These three groups are:

1. The intellectual, or, as they are better termed, the "intellectualizing" resistances, corresponding to the intellectual "working through" of the analytic material.

2. The transference resistances (especially the "acting out" which remains so puzzling to us)—in many cases the central task of analytic endeavor.

3. Those resistances which are connected with the *recollecting* of infantile material.

For the present discussion I have chosen the "intellectual forms of defense"—in spite of the greater fascination which the problem of "acting out" usually exerts.

The meaning of "intellectual resistances" may be formulated shortly as follows. In place of positive efforts to help in the process of intellectually working over the material, the patient seeks to force his analysis in that one direction alone and to substitute for analytic *experiencing* either an ostensibly affirmative "understanding" or a negative criticism.

If, then, we run through our "intellectualizing" patients in our mind, my impression is that we shall find the following types:

(*a*) Highly intellectual individuals of a genuinely sublimated sort who are able to place the good weapons at their command more or less extensively at the service of their resistances. Against this method of defense by the patient we have no *direct* means of attack. Although at one time the sublimation was a help to the defensive forces, it has in the course of time acquired mental elements (such as perceptual contents, talents, etc.) which contain material foreign to the analysis.

(*b*) Obsessional neurotics, whose intellectual resistances are well known to us in the form of direct "reaction formations" and "isolations."

(*c*) Patients with blocked or disturbed affects, who, having repressed the affective side of their life, have retained the intellectual side as the sole means of expressing their mental personality.

Analysis has been shown to be especially difficult in the case of these three types of resistance. For the patients obtain from their defense a "secondary gain" of narcissistic satisfaction and have so much the less reason for renouncing this mode of defense.

More amenable to analytic treatment are those intellectual resistances whose role as a process of defense reveals itself in two directions: (1) when they themselves are already affected by neurotic disturbance, and (2) when they constantly reappear in the analytic treatment at the point at which an objectionable instinctual impulse or an unwelcome affect threatens to present itself. The usual technique of the analyst, which consists either in not entering into intellectual argumentation at all or in seeking to invalidate the defense by pointing out its narcissistic tendencies, is here completely useless.

An approach to the resistance from the side hostile to the ego, that is, from the side where what is being warded off is situated, is frequently found to be quite inadequate. This is not to be wondered at, since the difficulty consists precisely in the ability of the ego to master promptly by intellectual means the warded off material and thus to effect a reinforced resistance to it. We must therefore make a direct attack on the defensive process itself; but we can be successful in this only if we have thoroughly grasped the nature of that process.

The analysis of a defensive process is possible only under one condition: there must be a weak spot in it somewhere, so that it gradually takes on the character of a symptom, or so that in some form it comes into conflict with the re-mainder of the ego.

It may also happen that the defensive process takes on a very complicated character, being carried out in several steps, and that what is pathological and unsuccessful in the patient is to be sought precisely in that place where every-thing appears to be functioning well and to the advantage of the ego.

Let me illustrate this by an example. A 45-year-old man in a prominent and responsible position was sent for an analytic exploration of his peculiar state. Whether he was suffering from a neurosis or not was still uncertain. For several months he and his friends had observed that his men-tal abilities had been losing ground. It was a question of a progressive weakening of his powers of mental retention.

This became so noticeable that suspicions of the beginning of a general paralysis were aroused. Although the physical findings were negative throughout, the presence of some organic disease of the brain still seemed most probable. The patient himself said that he felt his intellectual defect very intensely, but that he had the impression that the disturbance of his powers of retention existed in isolation from the remainder of his mental faculties. He was working with especial ease and increased interest on some scientific problems and hoped soon to be able to publish the results. This claim could not be diagnosed as a tendency to paralytic ideas of grandeur, for the patient was already a prominent publicist.

During the treatment I observed that the patient was very eager to interest me in material belonging to his past and produced present-day material only in so far as it concerned his erotic life. As soon as he approached his professional or scientific interests he would avoid the subject with the excuse that it was not worth while and that he knew that patients spoke about professional and scientific matters chiefly in order to avoid the more important affective ones. For the patient knew a great deal about analysis and the theory of its technique.

The analyst often finds himself forced to give up the technical routine of analysis and to let himself be guided by intuition. It was easier to do so in this case precisely because my patient's difficulties lay in the intellectual sphere. I insisted the more energetically on dealing with the intellectual side as the patient had really been sent for diagnostic purposes and there could be no question of a long analysis. I soon discovered that his loss of retentive powers related only to scientific matters, and principally to what he had just read. To obtain a clearer picture of his mental life I asked him to bring me his latest manuscripts and to discuss with me the problems contained in them. I will give you a short résumé of the results of a couple of weeks' investigation. For some years the patient had had a very intense friendship with another man whose great scientific talents had always greatly impressed him. The fields of interest of the two friends, while closely related, did not create a situation of rivalry. The friend was a pure theoretician, while my patient took a more practical interest in the field of education. But owing to certain professional circumstances my patient too was forced more into the theoretical field. His latent homosexual aggressiveness against his friend and his burning envy of him underwent repression, and my patient now discovered the following complicated method of defense. Through identification on the one hand and an aggressive "taking away" on the other, he appropriated the thoughts of his friend. These thoughts were known to him in part from his friend's publications and in part from private discussions. In order to deny, however, the unconscious plagiarism, he forgot everything which he had read or had heard from his friend; and he extended this mode of behavior to other fields of activity. This disturbance of mental retentiveness, which has the same structure as a parapraxis such as forgetting a word, is a very interesting phenomenon.

But in my patient the process of defense did not stop at the disturbance of his retentive powers. A careful examination of his theoretic productions showed that his unconscious plagiarism referred not only to his thoughts but to his creative efforts. His scientific work turned out to be an ingenious piecing together of ideas which his friend had already put in writing. The disturbance of his retentiveness served only as a preliminary step to this plagiarism, which could be successful only because he had "forgotten" what his friend had already said.

The discovery of this complicated process did not take place at the point which was felt to be pathological, i.e., in the patient's weakness of memory, but in the activity which had been taken for a successful sublimation, i.e., in his apparently undisturbed scientific achievements.

The patient was very much shaken by this discovery, for the process had been completely unconscious to him. I myself saw in this situation yet one more example of those paradoxes with which analysis has to struggle. In general we refuse to take an interest in the patient's case in so far as it regards his purely intellectual preoccupations, and consider it as a resistance when he seeks to guide the analysis in this direction. In matters of the intellect we are interested in his disturbances only in so far as they hide an inhibition or a symptom. His sublimations, so long as they are successful, lie outside our interests.

The patient whom we have been discussing should be a warning to us. For it often happens that what was regarded as a successful sublimation turns out to be an unsuccessful defensive process; and—as in this case—it may be only because the apparently successful activity seeks to creep behind a wall of resistance that the analyst's attention is attracted toward it. In psychoanalysis there are no hard and fast rules.

In the analytic unraveling of an intellectual defensive process of this kind it seems to become clear that the defense itself conforms in its structure to a neurotic symptom, that is, that there are contained in it not only an ascetic trend directed against the instinctual danger, but also an affirmative and gratificatory one, though in this case it is quite unconscious.

I should like to give another example to illustrate what I have been saying. An especially intelligent woman came to me for analysis on account of professional difficulties; these consisted in a purely intellectual inhibition of her scientific abilities. Her principal resistance showed itself in the constant efforts she made to give her analysis a didactic, intellectual character. But in the end, with the help of the transference, the analysis was successfully converted into an emotional experience and led to a good therapeutic result.

After her analysis, the patient provided an interesting epilogue to it. She declared that she had not the slightest recollection of the material which had come up during her analysis. This was all the more strange in a patient who had so thoroughly worked over her analysis on intellectual lines. In addition, she believed that her own efforts as an analyst were less successful than they might have been, because she was too much inclined to carry the analysis on to the intellectual plane.

The situation, which became quite clear in the analysis, was that since her childhood she had had to struggle against an especially strong sexual curiosity and against active tendencies to make sexual investigations. This curiosity was opposed by strong external and internal prohibitions. The rejected strivings were continued in the sublimated form of her intellectual proclivities—the defense thus received its specific character from the nature of that which had been warded off.

Analysis had indeed helped the patient to revive and deal with the sexual investigations hidden behind the defense; at the same time, however, my opposition to any "intellectualizing" on her part, which had the effect of a prohibition, repeated the prohibiting attitude of her very ascetic childhood environment. After the analysis—in deferred obedience—we see the old process being repeated. She renounced "knowledge" exactly like the child who apparently accepts sexual enlightenment only promptly to repress it once again.

But the fact that she sought to "intellectualize" with her own analysands originated in another unconscious motive. This "intellectualizing" was not only a sublimation of her infantile sexual curiosity, but also represented an identification with her father. She followed the same profession as he and was interested in the same kind of scientific work. Before her analytic treatment she had come to grief over this process of identification because of the fact that she was a girl and found her activities hampered by the anatomical difference.

Anna Freud regards the tendency to intellectualization in puberty as an effort of the ego to master the instincts with the aid of thought processes. According to my view, this form of defense appears only in those young people in whom *specific* instinctual tendencies in early childhood have already prepared a defensive process of this kind, and in such a manner that that process can cover a gratification of instinct. In the case of our patient it was sexual curiosity and everything connected with it which was indirectly gratified by the "intellectualization."

But to a defensive process of this type, formed early in life, there must be added, according to my observations, a later factor before this form of defense can be established and fixated. In the case under discussion this factor was the patient's identification with her father. I believe that it is these later factors which are decisive for the further development of the intellectualizing tendencies of puberty.

At this point I should like to make an observation which

is not directly connected with my theme, but offers a contribution to the problem of the influence of affective factors on retentive memory.

It is considered to be an established fact that the presbyophrenic phenomena of defects of memory are of an organic nature and show themselves purely in the intellectual sphere. In this connection I have been following up for some time a fact which came to my notice by chance. This is that the frequently increased ability of the presenile to recall memories from their more distant past does not appear to confine itself to conscious material. Childhood experiences, and fantasies, which have been excluded from consciousness all through life, often spring up spontaneously with great plasticity. My patient's old grandmother, a very puritanical and sexually repressed woman, acknowledged her sympathy for analysis when she recalled, in her seventieth year, Œdipus fantasies and sexual experiences which she had forgotten all her life. My further observations appear to show that there is an early stage of presbyophrenia, in which material which has up till then been unconscious is remembered as well.

I am inclined to suppose that this process originates when the ego, in renouncing sexual wishes, can also give up those inhibitions and resistances which it had built up against dangers that now no longer exist. Although this theory may be wrong, the observation underlying it is certainly true.

Closely related to the "intellectualizing" form of those defensive processes which express themselves as a resistance, is another form—that of "rationalization" or turning to reality.

I assume that in a patient with this sort of defensive

processes what has happened is that he has successfully disposed of his entire anxiety in regard to his internal institutions by avoiding them. He has simply fled from the gloomy world of his mental life into reality; and he proceeds to utilize reality as a defense against the analytic evocation of the ghosts which he has successfully dispelled. In consequence he hastens to translate the interpretations in analysis into the language of material reality. Thus figures of speech, symbols, and psychical reality are alien to him even when he does accept them intellectually and understands them. In his analysis he sometimes gives the impression of being stupid, sometimes of making fun of the treatment. But one soon discovers that it is a question of resistance and that he is making use of a form of defense which has freed him from anxiety on former occasions.

Here is an example of what I mean. A well educated man, who was pursuing active studies in the natural sciences, had turned his attention to experimentation with great keenness and would accept as "science" only that which could be objectively demonstrated—was written in black on white, as it were. Science was to him a collocation of facts. Hypotheses, problems and everything that is not directly demonstrable, he called "poetry but not science," and declared that he would have nothing to do with such matters.

He rejected analytic interpretations as "not demonstrable," and sought to invalidate his transference experience through argumentation. In this way he often succeeded in struggling successfully against his anxiety states, for quite a long while; but in the end they overpowered him and made the treatment possible.

The patient was the last child in the family. He was born

two months after the death of his father. There was a great deal of filial feeling in his family circle and he was extremely envious of his older brothers and sisters because they had known, and been loved by, his father. He entertained fantasies full of longing and—encouraged by his nurse—hoped some day to see his father as a ghost. Yet later this expectation was transferred into a fear. His energetic mother freed him from the influence of this nurse and the patient found consolation and help in his mother's assurance that there were no such things as ghosts, that no one had ever seen one yet and that death was decay and irrevocable annihilation.

Now we can understand, I think, the sources from which his turning to reality sprang and his denial of things which were not "materially" demonstrable.

This patient's attitude was determined by a quite individually colored prehistory. But exactly the same reactions and defensive processes can, as observation shows, also be turned against the ghosts which dwell within the subject and which threaten to return.

Another patient of mine exhibited a still more "realistic" mode of behavior. He concerned himself only with things which were useful, was interested in culture only because, after all, one had to "do what the others did" and let himself be analyzed because afterwards he could make more money and better his position.

In the analysis he showed himself unable to link his mental phenomena with a verbally conscious comprehension of them, as will be seen from his attitude to his dreams and their interpretation. He dreamed that a strikingly beautiful youth was revealed on closer inspection to be a hateful hairy ape with frightfully long arms. His associations pointed very clearly to his conflict over masturbation as well as to the identity of the ape with his own person. He understood and accepted this interpretation, yet the next day he repudiated it because he had seen in the mirror that he was not hairy at all and the measurement of his arms showed that they were much shorter than the ape's—consequently he could not be the ape.

After the interpretation of another dream, in which I was able to show him his negative transference as revealed in the identification of myself with a deceitful old fruit seller, he inquired of common acquaintances about my honesty, so as to prove to himself and to me that my interpretation possessed no reality value whatsoever.

This patient, too, had—as his analysis showed—learned early on in life to set up against his internal anxieties a reality which was innocuous because he could record and check up on it.

There was in him no trace of a Don Quixote who, carried along by the force of his illusions, of the unreal, would translate them into his life. Much rather was he a Sancho Panza; for he gave everything which was unreal, fantastic, or spiritual, the character of the crudely real. Reality gave him protection and enabled him to obtain satisfactions which were not prohibited.

We assume that this type of defense as we observe it in our patient had originated in that period in which the anxiety of the child was directed to the external world and in which the testing of reality had at the same time the effect of freeing him from anxiety, like a game in which the father, disguised as a wolf, cries out in order to quiet the mounting anxiety of the child: "But look, that's not a wolf, it's papa." Hence it appears as if reality testing and adaptation to reality not only originate under the pressure of necessity, but also as a consequence of their function in freeing from anxiety.

This method, already prepared in childhood, for gaining freedom from anxiety seems to me to be especially operative in the prepubertal stage before the onset of the genital trends. From analytic experience I have the impression that it serves chiefly for defense against the newly mobilized activity of fantasies and that it represents a defense form which is more complete and more ominous than "intellectualization." While in the latter case the function of affect and fantasy is replaced by intellect, in the former the thinking process itself is limited and the fear of fantasies is transferred to the fear of thinking.

A typical example is the gifted twelve-year-old boy, with his head full of fantastic plans for the future, who suddenly exclaims that he wants first of all to prove, as a common worker in a factory, which of his chemical and physical ideas can be realized. This boy is a youthful forerunner of a certain kind of specialists who are to be found as group products in some civilized societies. My first patient, in his clearly neurotic structure, is a prototype of such a group. I think we may expect to find certain civilizations which are deeply imbued with this particular form of defense against anxiety. These reactions may be deflected in one direction—for example in that of scientific research so that the unreal, the poetic and the mystical are represented to excess in art, religion, and philosophies of life. I believe that too forcible an education on lines of reality strongly reinforces this defense mechanism. This was the case with my last patient cited above.

From the point of view of the technical art of the analyst there arise here great difficulties. For, so long as he has not shattered the "reality values" of the patient, his efforts are almost hopeless, and in doing so he is going contrary to the analytic task of making the patient adapted to reality.

In complete contrast to the "realization" type, there is another type of patient whose characteristic is an especial intuition for his own internal processes, a striking gift for "internal perception." So far as I know them, this kind of patient comes as a candidate for training in analysis and gives the impression of having a particular psychological aptitude for the profession of analyst.

Closer observation shows, however, that this acuteness of "internal perception," which strikes us as a talent, is in fact a defensive process. We find that the patient (or candidate) lives in a severe anxiety state, which has neither a phobic nor yet a "free floating" character. It gives the impression, rather, of a state of rigidity from panic. The main way in which the internal anxiety finds expression is in numerous anxiety dreams of a persecutory character. The patient works brilliantly in the first phase of the analysis, sees and understands things which are usually unconscious and takes away from the analyst every possibility of interfering in his analysis. This activity which is forcibly directed on to his internal life goes along with a markedly passive attitude toward the real world about him. These patients are more or less adapted to reality, but they do not exert much will power and allow themselves to be dominated by men and circumstances.

Their internal perception is gradually revealed as a sharpened self-observation with the aim of defending against internal dangers. They are like a timid listener in the dark who perceives sounds more clearly. One of these patients actually told me that he observed himself so exactly "so as not to go insane." This introspection always becomes intensified when the transference becomes stronger and the understanding collaboration of the analyst more dangerous. Gradually this defense becomes unsatisfactory and the anxiety takes on more and more a transference character. In one case it was transformed into a paranoid attitude to the analyst. One could observe *in statu nascendi* the process of transformation from "internal perception" to the "hostile observer" in the external world. Whether this is a question of the reinforcement and breaking through of repressed instinctual tendencies, which provoke by an anxiety signal the defending forces of self-observation, or whether it is primarily a matter of an increased activity of the ego or superego, remains at present an open question.

This process certainly has analogies with hypochondria and depersonalization (in Schilder's sense), in which also an attempt is made to objectify and master rejected mental contents by means of self-observation.

The line of demarcation between the positive and the pathological functioning of such an "intuitive" attitude is not clear-cut. Where this attitude takes on more and more the character of a resistance in the analysis we are led on the one hand to think of the familiar clairvoyance of the schizophrenic, and on the other to take into consideration the possibility of a preliminary stage of a paranoid process.

I have, for the present, set up three forms of "internal perception."

1. A purely positive achievement on the part of the observing portion of the ego without pathological reaction, which is therefore not an object of direct analytical treatment, even when it is used as a defense.

2. An endophobia, i.e., a phobia of the internal part of

the self, in which the strengthened introspection affords freedom from anxiety but with internal restrictions.

3. Paranoia turned against the inner self, in which the introspecting ego is felt as something strange and so plays the part of persecutor. The comprehension of this type leads directly to the problem of depersonalization and other forms of schizoid reaction, but is not the theme of my paper.

I have attempted to show how a specific way of reacting of the ego, which began as a defense mechanism, can either become an immovable and positive possession of the mental apparatus, or merely form a thin veil over the subject's neurotic fears—a veil which must be drawn away by analysis in order to allow what it conceals to be dealt with.

I have brought forward a few types to show that something that has hitherto been of positive value in the ego can be made to serve a negative purpose during the analysis and that it must be destroyed by the process of analysis; but that this should only be done if there is a possibility of creating a better economy in the mental life of the individual. Whether such a possibility exists or not is a question which analytic experience and tact alone can decide.

This paper was first read before the Fourteenth International Psycho-Analytical Congress at Marienbad in 1936. It was published under the title "Uber bestimmte Widerstandsformen" in the *Internationale Zeitschrift für Psychoanalyse*, Vol. XXIV, 1939, and appeared in English in the *International Journal of Psycho-Analysis*, Vol. XX, 1939. The translator is unknown.

Helene Deutsch became well-known for her work, *The Psychology of Women*, which is still considered a classic in psychoanalytic literature. She also wrote extensively on female homosexuality.

The early development of conscience in the child

Melanie Klein

One of the most important contributions of psychoanalytic research has been the discovery of the mental processes which underlie the development of conscience in the individual. In his work of bringing to light unconscious instinctual tendencies, Freud has also recognized the existence of those forces which serve as a defense against them. According to his findings, which psychoanalytic practice has borne out in every instance, the person's conscience is a precipitate or representative of his early relations to his parents. He has in some sense internalized his parents—has taken them into himself. There they become a differentiated part of his ego—his superego—and an agency which advances against the rest of his ego certain requirements, reproaches, and admonitions, and which stands in opposition to his instinctual impulses.

Freud has since shown that the operation of this superego is not limited to the conscious mind, is not only what is meant by conscience, but also exerts an unconscious and often very oppressive influence which is an important factor both in mental illness and in the development of normal personality. This new discovery has brought the study of

the superego and its origins more and more into the focus
of psychoanalytic investigation.

In the course of my analysis of small children, as I began
to get a direct knowledge of the foundations upon which
their superego was built, I came upon certain facts which
seemed to allow of an enlargement in some directions of
Freud's theory on this subject. There could be no doubt
that a superego had been in full operation for some time
in my small patients of between two and three quarters
and four years of age, whereas according to the accepted
view the superego did not begin to be activated until the
Œdipus complex had died down—i.e., until about the fifth
year of life. Furthermore, my data showed that this early
superego was immeasurably harsher and more cruel than
that of the older child or adult, and that it literally crushed
down the feeble ego of the small child.

In the adult, it is true, we find a superego at work which
is a great deal more severe than the subject's parents were
in reality, and which is in other ways by no means identical
with them.[1] Nevertheless it approximates to them more or
less. But in the small child we come across a superego
of the most incredible and fantastic character. And the
younger the child is, or the deeper the mental level we
penetrate to, the more this is the case. We get to look upon
the child's fear of being devoured, or cut up, or torn to
pieces, or its terror of being surrounded and pursued by
menacing figures, as a regular component of its mental
life; and we know that the man-eating wolf, the fire-spew-

---

[1] In *Symposium on Child Analysis*, similar views, based on adult
analysis and seen from somewhat different angles, were put forward
by Ernest Jones, Mrs. Rivière, Edward Glover, and Miss Searl
Miss Searl has also had her view confirmed by her experiences of
child analysis.

ing dragon, and all the evil monsters out of myths and fairy stories flourish and exert their unconscious influence in the fantasy of each individual child, and it feels itself persecuted and threatened by those evil shapes. But I think we can know more than this. I have no doubt from my own analytic observations that the identities behind those imaginary, terrifying figures are the child's own parents, and that those dreadful shapes in some way or other reflect the features of its father and mother, however distorted and fantastic the resemblance may be.

If we accept these facts of early analytic observation and recognize that the things the child fears are these internalized wild beasts and monsters which it equates with its parents, we are led to the following conclusions: (1) The superego of the child does not coincide with the picture presented by its real parents, but is created out of imaginary pictures or *imagos* of them which it has taken up into itself; (2) Its fear of real objects—its phobic anxiety—is based upon its fear both of its unrealistic superego and of objects which are real in themselves, but which it views in a fantastic light under the influence of its superego.

This brings us to the problem which seems to me to be the central one in the whole question of superego formation. How does it come about that the child creates such a fantastic image of its parents—an image that is so far removed from reality? The answer is to be found in the facts elicited in early analysis. In penetrating to the deepest layers of the child's mind and discovering those enormous quantities of anxiety—those fears of imaginary objects and those terrors of being attacked in all sorts of ways—we also lay bare a corresponding amount of repressed impulses of aggression, and can observe the causal connection which exists between the child's fears and its aggressive tendencies.

In his book, *Beyond the Pleasure Principle,* Freud puts forward a theory according to which at the outset of the life of the human organism the instinct of aggression, or death instinct, is being opposed and bound down by the libido, or life instinct—the eros. A fusion of the two instincts ensues, and gives rise to sadism. In order to escape from being destroyed by its own death instinct, the organism employs its narcissistic, or self-regarding, libido to force the former outward, and direct it against its objects. Freud considers this process as fundamental for the person's sadistic relations to his objects. I should say, moreover, that parallel with this deflection of the death instinct outward against objects, an intra-psychic reaction of defense goes on against that part of the instinct which could not be thus externalized. For the danger of being destroyed by this instinct of aggression sets up, I think, an excessive tension in the ego, which is felt by it as an anxiety,[2] so that it is faced at the very beginning of its development with the task of mobilizing libido against its death instinct. It can, however, only imperfectly fulfill this task, since, owing to the fusion of the two instincts, it can no longer, as we know, effect a separation between them. A division takes place in the id, or instinctual levels of the psyche, by which one part of the instinctual impulses is directed against the other.

This apparently earliest measure of defense on the part of the ego constitutes, I think, the foundation stone of the development of the superego, whose excessive violence in this early stage would thus be accounted for by the fact

---

[2] This tension is, it is true, felt as a libidinal tension as well, since the destructive and libidinal instincts are fused together; but its effect of causing anxiety is referable, in my opinion, to the destructive components in it

that it is an offshoot of very intense destructive instincts, and contains, along with a certain proportion of libidinal impulses, very large quantities of aggressive ones.[3]

This view of the matter makes it also less puzzling to understand why the child should form such monstrous and fantastic images of his parents. For he perceives his anxiety arising from his aggressive instincts as fear of an external object, both because he has made that object their outward goal, and because he has projected them on to it so that they seem to be initiated against himself from that quarter.[4]

He thus displaces the source of his anxiety outwards and turns his objects into dangerous ones; but, ultimately, that danger belongs to his own aggressive instincts. For this reason his fear of his objects will always be proportionate to the degree of his own sadistic impulses.

It is not, however, simply a question of converting a given amount of sadism into a corresponding amount of anxiety. The relation is one of content as well. The child's fear of its object and the imaginary attacks it will suffer from it adhere in every detail to the particular aggressive impulses and fantasies which it harbors against its environment. In this way each child develops parental *imagos* that are peculiar to itself; though in every case they will be of an unreal and terrifying character.

According to my observations, the formation of the superego begins at the same time as the child makes its

---

[3] In his *Civilization and Its Discontents* Freud says: . . . "that the original severity of the superego does not—or not so much—represent the severity which has been experienced or anticipated from the object, but expresses the child's own aggressiveness toward the latter."

[4] The infant has, incidentally, some real grounds for fearing its mother, since it becomes growingly aware that she has the power to grant or withhold the gratification of its needs.

earliest oral introjection of its objects.[5] Since the first *imagos* it thus forms are endowed with all the attributes of the intense sadism belonging to this stage of its development, and since they will once more be projected on to objects of the outer world, the small child becomes dominated by the fear of suffering unimaginable cruel attacks, both from its real objects and from its superego. Its anxiety will serve to increase its own sadistic impulses by urging it to destroy those hostile objects so as to escape their onslaughts. The vicious circle that is thus set up, in which the child's anxiety impels it to destroy its object, results in an increase of its own anxiety, and this once again urges it on against its object, and constitutes a psychological mechanism which, in my view, is at the bottom of asocial and criminal tendencies in the individual. Thus, we must assume that it is the excessive severity and overpowering cruelty of the superego, not the weakness or want of it, as is usually supposed, which is responsible for the behavior of asocial and criminal persons.

In a somewhat later stage of development, fear of the superego will cause the ego to turn away from the anxiety-arousing object. This defensive mechanism can lead to a defective or impaired object relation on the part of the child.

As we know, when the genital stage sets in, the child's sadistic instincts have normally been overcome, and its relationship to objects have acquired a positive character. In

---

[5] This view is also based on my belief that the child's Œdipus tendencies, too, begin much earlier than has hitherto been thought, i.e., while it is still in the suckling stage, long before its genital impulses have become paramount. In my opinion the child incorporates its Œdipus objects during the oral-sadistic stage, and it is at this time, in close connexion with its earliest Œdipus impulses, that its superego begins to develop.

my view such an advance in its development accompanies and interacts with alterations in the nature of its superego. For the more the child's sadism is lessened, the more the influence of its unreal and frightening *imagos* recedes into the background, since they are the offshoots of its own aggressive tendencies. And as its genital impulses grow in strength there emerge beneficent and helpful *imagos*, based upon its fixations, in the oral-sucking stage, on its generous and kindly mother, which approximate more closely to the real objects; and its superego, from being a threatening, despotic force issuing senseless and self-contradictory commands which the ego is totally unable to satisfy, begins to exert a milder and more persuasive rule and to make requirements which are capable of being fulfilled. In fact, it gradually becomes transformed into conscience in the true sense of the word.

As the character of the superego varies, moreover, so will its effect upon the ego and the defensive mechanism it sets in motion there. We know from Freud that pity is a reaction to cruelty. But reactions of this kind do not set in until the child has attained some degree of positive object relationship—until, in other words, its genital organization has come to the front. If we place this fact side by side with the facts concerning the formation of the superego, as I see them, we shall be able to come to the following conclusions: so long as the function of the superego is mainly to arouse anxiety it will call out those violent defensive mechanisms in the ego which we have described above, and which are unethical and asocial in their nature. But as soon as the child's sadism is diminished and the character and function of its superego changed so that it arouses less anxiety and more sense of guilt, those defensive mechanisms which form the basis of a moral and ethical attitude are activated, and the child begins to have consideration for its objects, and to be amenable to social feeling.[6]

Numerous analyses of children of all ages have borne out this view. In play analysis we are able to follow the course of our patients' fantasies as represented in their games and play, and to establish a connection between those fantasies and their anxiety. As we proceed to analyze the content of their anxiety, we see the aggressive tendencies and fantasies which give rise to it come forward more and more, and grow to huge proportions, both in amount and intensity. The ego of the small child is in danger of being over-whelmed by their elemental force and enormous extent, and is engaged in a perpetual struggle to maintain itself against them with the help of its libidinal impulses, either by holding them under, or calming them down, or render-ing them innocuous.

This picture exemplifies Freud's thesis of the life instincts (eros) at war with the death instincts, or instincts of ag-gression. But we also recognize that there is the closest union and interaction between those two forces at every point, so that analysis can only succeed in tracing the child's aggressive fantasies in all their details, and thus diminishing their effect, in so far as it can follow up the libidinal ones and uncover their earliest sources as well—and vice versa.

Concerning the actual content and aims of those fan-tasies, we know from Freud and Abraham that in the earliest, pregenital stages of libidinal organization, in which

---

[6] In analyzing adults it was for the most part only these later functions and attributes of the superego that came under notice. Analysts were therefore inclined to regard them as constituting its specific character; and, indeed, only recognized the superego as such in so far as it appeared in this character.

this fusion of libido and destructive instinct takes place, the sadistic impulses of the child are paramount. As the analysis of every grown-up person demonstrates, in the oral-sadistic stage which follows upon the oral-sucking one, the small child goes through a cannibalistic phase with which are associated a wealth of cannibalistic fantasies. These fantasies, although they are still centered round eating up the mother's breast or her whole person, are not solely concerned with the gratification of a primitive desire for nourishment. They also serve to gratify the child's destructive impulses. The sadistic phase which succeeds to this—the anal-sadistic phase—is characterized by a dominating interest in excretory processes—in feces and the anus; and this interest too, is closely allied to extremely strong destructive tendencies.[7]

We know that the ejection of feces symbolizes a forcible ejection of the incorporated object and is accompanied with feelings of hostility and cruelty, and with destructive desires of various kinds, the buttocks receiving importance as an object of those activities. In my opinion, however, the anal-sadistic tendencies contain more profound and deeply repressed aims and objects still. The data I have been able to collect from early analyses show that between the oral-sadistic and anal-sadistic tendencies there is inserted a stage in which urethral-sadistic tendencies make themselves felt, and that the anal and urethral tendencies are a direct continuation of the oral-sadistic ones as regards the specific aim and object of attack. In its oral-sadistic fantasies the child attacks its mother's breast, and the means it employs

---

[7] Besides Freud, Jones, Abraham, and Ferenczi have been the chief contributors to our knowledge of the influence this alliance has exerted upon character formation and neurosis in the individual.

are its teeth and jaws. In its urethral and anal fantasies it seeks to destroy the inside of the mother's body, and uses its urine and feces for this purpose. In this second group of fantasies the excrements are regarded as burning and corroding substances, wild animals, weapons of all kinds, etc.; and the child enters a phase in which it directs every instrument of its sadism to the one purpose of destroying its mother's body and what is contained in it.

As regards choice of object, the child's oral-sadistic impulses are still the underlying factor, so that it thinks of sucking out and eating up the inside of its mother's body as though it were a breast. But those impulses receive an extension from the child's first sexual theories, which it develops during this phase. We already knew that when its genital instincts awakened it began to have unconscious theories about copulation between its parents, birth of children, etc. But early analysis has shown that it develops such theories much earlier than this, at a time when its pregenital impulses still mainly determine their character, though its as yet concealed genital impulses have some say in the matter. These theories are to the effect that in copulation the mother is continually incorporating the father's penis via the mouth, so that her body is filled with a great many penises and babies. All these the child desires to eat up and destroy.

In attacking its mother's inside, therefore, the child is attacking a great number of objects, and is embarking on a course which is fraught with consequences. The womb first stands for the world; and the child originally approaches this world with desires to attack and destroy it, and is therefore prepared from the outset to view the real, external world as more or less hostile to itself, and peopled

with objects ready to make attacks upon it.[8] Its belief that
in thus attacking its mother's body it has also attacked its
father and its brothers and sisters, and, in a wider sense, the
whole world, is, in my experience, one of the underlying
causes of its sense of guilt, and of the development of its
social and moral feelings in general.[9] For when the excessive
severity of the superego has become somewhat lessened,
its visitations upon the ego on account of those imaginary
attacks induce feelings of guilt which arouse strong tendencies in the child to make good the imaginary damage it
has done to its objects. And now the individual content
and details of its destructive fantasies help to determine the
development of its sublimations, which indirectly subserve
its restitutive tendencies,[10] or to produce even more direct
desires to help other people.

Play analyses show that when the child's aggressive instincts are at their height it never tires of tearing and cutting up, breaking, wetting, and burning all sorts of things
like paper, matches, boxes, small toys, all of which represent its parents and brothers and sisters, and its mother's

---

[8] An excessive strength of such early anxiety situations is, in my
opinion, a fundamental factor in the production of psychotic disorders.

[9] Owing to the child's belief in the omnipotence of thoughts (cf.
Freud, *Totem and Taboo;* Ferenczi, *Development of the Sense of
Reality*)—a belief dating from an earlier stage of development—it
confuses its imaginary attacks with real ones; and the consequences
of this can still be seen at work in adult life.

[10] In my article, "Infantile Anxiety Situations Reflected in a
Work of Art and in the Creative Instinct," I have maintained that
the person's sense of guilt and desire to restore the damaged object are a universal and fundamental factor in the development
of his sublimations. Miss Sharpe in her paper, "Certain Aspects of
Sublimation and Delusion," has come to the same conclusions.

body and breasts, and that this rage for destruction alternates with attacks of anxiety and a sense of guilt. But when, in the course of analysis, anxiety slowly diminishes, its constructive tendencies begin to come to the fore.[11] For instance, where before a small boy has done nothing but chop bits of wood to pieces, he will now begin to try and make those bits of wood into a pencil. He will take pieces of lead got from pencils he has cut up, and put them in a crack in the wood, and then sew a piece of stuff round the rough wood to make it look nicer. That this homemade pencil represents his father's penis, which he has destroyed in fantasy, and his own, whose destruction he dreads as a measure of retaliation, is evident, furthermore, from the general context of the material he presents, and from the associations he gives to it.

When, in the course of its analysis, the child begins to show stronger constructive tendencies in all sorts of ways in its play and its sublimations—painting or writing or drawing things instead of smearing everything with ashes, or sewing and designing where it used to cut up or tear to pieces—it also exhibits changes in its relation to its father or mother, or to its brothers and sisters; and these changes mark the beginning of an improved object relationship in general, and a growth of social feeling. What channels of sublimation will become open to the child, how powerful will be its impulsions to make restitution, and what forms they will assume—these things are determined not only by the extent of its primary aggressive tendencies, but by the interplay of a number of other factors which we have no room to discuss in these pages. But our knowledge of child

[11] In analysis the resolution of anxiety is effected gradually and evenly, so that both it and the aggressive instincts are set free in duly apportioned quantities.

analysis allows us to say this much, that analysis of the deepest layers of the superego invariably leads to a considerable betterment in the child's object relationship, its capacity for sublimation, and its powers of social adaptation—that it makes the child not only happier and healthier in itself, but more capable of social and ethical feeling.

This brings us to the consideration of a very obvious objection that may be raised against child analysis. It might be asked, would not too great a reduction of the severity of the superego—a reduction below a certain favorable level—have an opposite result and lead to the abolition of social and ethical sentiments in the child? The answer to this is, in the first place, that so great a diminution has never, as far as I know, happened in fact; and, in the second place, that there are theoretical reasons for believing that it never can happen. As far as actual experience goes, we know that in analyzing the pregenital libidinal fixations we can only succeed in converting a certain amount of the libidinal quantities involved into genital libido, even in favorable circumstances, and that the remainder, and no unimportant remainder, continues to be operative as pregenital libido and sadism; although, since the genital level has now more firmly established its supremacy, it can be better dealt with by the ego, either by receiving satisfaction, or by being kept down, or by undergoing modification or sublimation. In the same way analysis can never entirely do away with the sadistic nucleus of the superego, which has been formed under the primacy of the pregenital levels; but it can mitigate it by increasing the strength of the genital level, so that the now more powerful ego can deal with its superego, as it does with its instinctual impulses, in a manner that shall be more satisfactory both for the individual himself and for the world about him.

So far we have been concerned to establish the fact that the social and moral feelings of the person develop from a superego of a milder type, governed by the genital level. Now we must consider the inferences that follow from this. The deeper analysis penetrates into the lower levels of the child's mind, the more will it succeed in mitigating the severity of the superego, by lessening the operation of its sadistic constituents that arise from the earliest stages of development. In doing this, analysis prepares the way not only for the achievement of social adaptability in the child, but for the development of moral and ethical standards in the adult; for a development of this kind depends upon both superego and sexuality having satisfactorily attained to a genital level at the close of the expansion of the child's sexual life,[12] so that the superego shall have developed the character and function from which the person's sense of guilt in so far as it is socially valuable—i.e., his conscience—is derived.

Experience has already for some time shown that psychoanalysis, though originally devised by Freud as a method of curing mental disease, accomplishes a second purpose as well. It puts right disturbances of character formation, especially in children and adolescents, where it is able to effect very considerable alterations. Indeed, we may say that after it has been analyzed every child exhibits radical changes of character; nor can we avoid the conviction, based on observation of fact, that character analysis is no less important than analysis of neuroses as a therapeutic measure.

In view of these facts, one cannot help wondering

[12] That is, when the latency period sets in—approximately between the ages of five and six.

whether psychoanalysis is not destined to go beyond the single individual in its range of operation and influence the life of mankind as a whole. The repeated attempts that have been made to improve humanity—in particular to make it more peaceable—have failed, because nobody has understood the full depth and vigor of the instincts of aggression innate in each individual. Such efforts do not seek to do more than encourage the positive, well-wishing impulses of the person while denying or suppressing his aggressive ones. And so they have been doomed to failure from the beginning. But psychoanalysis has different means at its disposal for a task of this kind. It cannot, it is true, altogether do away with man's aggressive instinct as such; but it can, by diminishing the anxiety which accentuates those instincts, break up the mutual reinforcement that is going on all the time between his hatred and his fear. When, in our analytic work, we are always seeing how the resolution of early infantile anxiety not only lessens and modifies the child's aggressive impulses, but leads to a more valuable employment and gratification of them from a social point of view; how the child shows an ever growing, deeply rooted desire to be loved and to love, and to be at peace with the world about it; and how much pleasure and benefit, and what a lessening of anxiety it derives from the fulfillment of this desire—when we see all this, we are ready to believe that what now would seem a Utopian state of things may well come true in those distant days when, as I hope, child analysis will become as much a part of every person's upbringing as school education is now. Then, perhaps, that hostile attitude, springing from fear and suspicion, which is latent more or less strongly in each human being, and which intensifies a hundredfold in him every impulse of destruction, will give way to kindlier and more trustful feelings toward his fellow men, and people may inhabit the world together in greater peace and goodwill than they do now.

BIBLIOGRAPHY

Abraham, Karl. "A Short Study of the Development of the Libido Viewed in the Light of Mental Disorders," tr. by Clement A. Douglas Bryan and Alix Strachey. *Selected Papers on Psychoanalysis.* New York: Basic Books, 1953.

————. "Contributions to the Theory of the Anal Character," tr. by Clement A. Douglas Bryan and Alix Strachey. *Selected Papers on Psychoanalysis.* New York: Basic Books, 1953.

Ferenczi, Sándor. "The Origin of the Interest in Money," tr. by Ernest Jones. *Contributions to Psychoanalysis.* New York: Basic Books, 1950.

————. "Stages of the Development of the Sense of Reality," tr. by Ernest Jones. *Contributions to Psychoanalysis.* New York: Basic Books, 1950.

Freud, Sigmund. *Group Psychology and the Analysis of the Ego.* Tr. by James Strachey. New York: Liveright, 1940.

————. *Totem and Taboo.* Tr. by James Strachey. New York: W. W. Norton, 1952.

————. "Character and Anal Erotism," tr. by R. C. M. McWatters. *Collected Papers,* II. New York: Basic Books, 1959.

————. *Beyond the Pleasure Principle.* Tr. by James Strachey. New York: W. W. Norton, 1961.

————. *The Ego and the Id.* Tr. by James Strachey. New York: W. W. Norton, 1962.

————. *Civilization and Its Discontents.* Tr. by James Strachey. New York: W. W. Norton, 1963.

————. *Three Contributions to the Theory of Sex.* Tr. by A. A. Brill. New York: E. P. Dutton, 1963.

Glover, Richard. "Symposium on Child Analysis," *International Journal of Psycho-Analysis,* VIII, 1927.

Jones, Ernest. "Hate and Anal Erotism in the Obsessional Neurosis," *Papers on Psychoanalysis.* Baltimore: Williams and Wilkins, 1950.

Klein, Melanie. "Symposium on Child Analysis," *International Journal of Psycho-Analysis,* VIII, 1927.

————. "Early Stages of the Oedipus Conflict," *International Journal of Psycho-Analysis*, IX, 1928.

————. "Infantile Anxiety Situations Reflected in a Work of Art and the Creative Impulse," *International Journal of Psycho-Analysis*, X, 1929.

————. "The Importance of Symbol Formation in the Development of the Ego," *International Journal of Psycho-Analysis*, XI, 1930.

Rivière, Joan. "Symposium on Child Analysis," *International Journal of Psycho-Analysis*, VIII, 1927.

Searl, M. N. "Symposium on Child Analysis," *International Journal of Psycho-Analysis*, VIII, 1927.

Sharpe, Ella F. "Certain Aspects of Sublimation and Delusion," *International Journal of Psycho-Analysis*, XI, 1930.

This paper first appeared in the *International Journal of Psycho-Analysis*, Vol. XI, 1930. It was later reprinted in Melanie Klein's *Contributions to Psycho-Analysis* (London: Hogarth, 1946; and New York: McGraw-Hill, 1964).

Melanie Klein is, with Anna Freud, one of the outstanding pioneers in child analysis. Her influence was especially felt in England where she played an important role in the British Psycho-Analytic Society.